CW00860104

C
Y

4 1 0008709 9

Sacred Space

M.E./C.F.S., Depression, Anxiety and Stress - A Guide to Healing and Recovery

Elizabeth Bailey
Reflexologist and Reiki Healer

Bloomington, IN   Milton Keynes, UK

authorHOUSE®

AuthorHouse™
1663 Liberty Drive, Suite 200
Bloomington, IN 47403
www.authorhouse.com
Phone: 1-800-839-8640

AuthorHouse™ UK Ltd.
500 Avebury Boulevard
Central Milton Keynes, MK9 2BE
www.authorhouse.co.uk
Phone: 08001974150

First published by AuthorHouse 12/29/2006

ISBN: 978-1-4259-8204-1(sc)

Printed in the United States of America
Bloomington, Indiana

This book is printed on acid-free paper.

For my son and soul mate
whose love and strength
gave me the inspiration to make this possible
with all of my love X

And in loving memory of my father Norman
and my dearest friend Trevor

Special Acknowledgements

My sincere love and thanks go to all the following Angels on Earth who helped to make this possible:

My darling Mum Joanie whose love and friendship I'll carry with me always *X*

Debbie my spiritual healer, truly an Angel in disguise! *X*

Mark my yoga teacher for his selfless help and guidance *X*

Martin my Reiki Master and teacher, for his love and the gift of Reiki, which helped me to deliver this to you *X*

Gabrielle for her generous and loving support in helping me with the editing of *'Sacred Space'* and for her beautiful design for the cover and who, like an angel, came to my rescue as if on cue! *X*

Sophie for her loving support and help with proof reading *X*

Paul for becoming even more of a domestic God overnight *X*

Jude for her open arms, words of wisdom, reassurance and love at such a special time *X*

Everyone at The Triangle Healing Trust for their love and support *X*

Joe of Sacred Spirits for his kindness and gentle encouragement, which helped me on my way *X*

Kate of Antique Maison, Arundel, West Sussex, for her generous support *X*

Everyone at Author House publishing who helped to make this possible *X*

And the beautiful and incredible children and staff at Great Walstead Pre-preparatory School in Lindfield, West Sussex, for their love and for enabling me to smile again from the inside out *XXX*

"There's not much than can beat a child holding your hand and showing you their love when the world around you is spinning so fast…."

Contents

Introduction

Just for a moment picture yourself having more energy, enthusiasm, feeling calmer and more peaceful. Imagine being able to turn your life around and follow your purpose so you can achieve your goals and having gained this through your own journey of self-healing. Well that's what happened to me. In 2003 and during the space of just four months, my son and I were both diagnosed as suffering from M.E. (Myalgic Encephalomyelitis) also known as C.F.S. (Chronic Fatigue Syndrome). By working our way through trauma and illness we discovered an enlightening path towards coping and recovery. The direction of our lives took an extraordinary turn, and we managed to achieve more than we ever dreamed possible.

I wrote 'Sacred Space' to share with everyone the proven natural healing methods which can help towards coping and recovery from M.E./C.F.S., depression, anxiety and stress related illness. Its purpose is that it should be used alongside conventional medical treatment so that even more wonderful things can take place.

I hope that it will pass on the sparks of light, which were handed to me, and bring inspiration and awareness, and assure you that with a *can do* approach it's possible to *positively* transform your life through your own journey of healing.

I've purposely kept it compact so you can dip into it whenever the mood takes you, and because I **know** how you must be feeling right now, it's very much written from the heart.

Some *wonderful* circumstances have lead me to write this book, which I shall tell you about shortly, and what an amazing journey it's been. I don't know **what** gave me the incredible **drive** to write, but I firmly believe that the words are very much needed during these times and most importantly, if it helps you, then it will have fulfilled its purpose.

Wishing you a speedy recovery,

With Love,

Liz

And he said unto them. Come ye yourselves apart into a desert place and rest a while; for there were many coming and going, and they had no leisure so much as to eat...

JESUS
St. Mark 6 7:31

The Journey So Far

During the past few months I have been shown great evidence of a 'spiritual need' occurring around us and have been given some wonderful opportunities. By working alongside the medical profession and bringing awareness of natural healing methods into many areas, I have seen some awe inspiring and magical things happen, which is so far away from how my life used to be before my son and I fell victims to M.E./C.F.S.

I have recently been involved with a local healing centre, which is a wonderful charity project that offers counselling, healing and support to anyone in need. It also provides a beautiful space for support groups who assist patients suffering from life threatening illnesses and I've felt both honoured and humbled to be a part of this incredible organisation. Volunteering to help at the centre turned out to be the start of the most *amazing transformation* that's occurred in my life so far.

Something else that became clear along the way is that I have been given the gift of meeting some wonderful people. Crucially, all these people have something remarkable in common. They have all experienced trauma in their lives, yet, they have come through bad times to be stronger, more compassionate, caring human beings who give advice freely. In addition, I have met a few *extra special* people who have faced life-threatening illness who have been my teachers along the way, all proof indeed that *what doesn't break you makes you stronger.*

When I decided to write a guidebook to healing and recovery I didn't particularly set out to write about spirituality, but since the circumstances which lead to the creation of this book are so important, I couldn't *possibly* leave them out!

In fact it all started after I'd received a few sessions of *spiritual healing*. I'd mentioned to a few people around me that I wanted to write a book about my experiences to help others, but didn't know if I had the energy. Then, as I practiced my relaxation and meditations and during my *quietest moments*, I realised that I was beginning to receive what I can only describe as *'messages'*; thoughts that would come to me whenever I asked a question in my mind. Strangely, it appeared that the 'answers' were coming back immediately and would drop into my mind clearer than ever before. It was as if someone was providing them, yet they weren't clearly audible and were received as very positive but gentle statements. The amazing thing was that they didn't reflect anything *like* I was really feeling at the time.

The process then became even more intriguing. I would go to bed at night only to be regularly woken anytime from about 11.30pm onwards to have thoughts about what should be included in my book! The messages got more persistent and sleep was impossible until I'd written down what was coming to me, so I ended up keeping a pen and notebook by my bedside!

When I told my spiritual healer Debbie about what was happening, she clapped her hands with delight, smiled her gorgeous smile and said in a *knowing* way, "Yes that's usually the time it happens, isn't it exciting!". It was all very new to me but, for the first time in my life, I felt like I was being driven, not in a bad way, but in a way I'd never experienced before and most importantly, it was at a time when I was *really* ready to listen.

Aside from the phenomenal amount of information I received when I least expected it regarding what I should include in the book, the other messages I received came through in beautiful worded sentences and certainly not in the words that I'd have chosen. I'm even a bit nervous about telling the world because I feel it's so private and I still don't know exactly why it was happening and *still is*. Also I slightly feared that the magic might go away!

As I began to put all the pieces of information together onto the computer the process began to speed up and more details kept coming. With regards to the contents of the book, they were facts from my past, which I already knew about but *it was as if a switch had been turned on inside me and it wouldn't let up until everything had been written down.* I'd sit for hours at a time working on the computer usually between 11pm to 2am, much to my family's dismay and amazement (mainly because they knew that I usually disliked working on computers, yet, suddenly I was loving every minute of it) and to this day I'll never know how I had the energy or indeed creativity to produce this book. Astonishingly, I must add, the first draft was also written and complete within just five weeks!

Just Before We Get Going

There shouldn't be any hard and fast rules for achieving anything 'good' in life, especially when it comes to healing.

The less tension there is in anything the more effective things can be, simply because there is *less resistance.*

We are human *BE-ings* not human *DO-ings* and we all need to top up our energies everyday and for the rest of our lives. When we learn to be open enough to discover our own mind, body and spiritual balance, it's possible that we can live happier, healthier, more fulfilling lives. Hopefully then, we can look back and realise just how far we've come in learning how to really live our lives to the full and accept that it's O.K. to sit quietly and simply just to 'be'.

This affirmation can be useful if you feel under pressure. You could write it on a few notes and place them around the house or at work to remind yourself every so often.

P - P R E S E R V E
A - A N D
C - C O N S E R V E
E - E N E R G I E S !

It's important to PACE ourselves when recovering from illness or coping with stress of any kind. It helps too when we can learn to become more attuned to being able to recognise the signs in our bodies to watch out for. By bringing awareness into our lives we can begin to recognise what our bodies are trying to tell us.

Learning to be *'open'* to finding out about ways to recover shows that we are in fact already well on the way to recovery.

To start to get our balance right again gentle graduated exercise as well as regular rest times are important in recovery, particularly as the vascular system is affected by M.E./C.F.S., depression, anxiety and stress. This can be an education for many of us who really should give ourselves a little more time to move about, yet, also just as importantly, learn to take time to completely and utterly relax like never before.

Through 'awareness' we can learn to ride the waves of life's ebbs and flows on their crest!

When you start my suggested recovery plan you may feel a little more tired initially, particularly at the beginning of this new routine. It's perfectly normal and to be expected. In fact, it's a fantastic sign to take note of because it positively indicates that your body is responding immediately and is beginning the natural process of healing.

Try to be patient with yourself along the way. As individual as we are, each one of us is unique in our healing responses and it's important to view coping and recovery that way.

A fantastic way to ground yourself and prepare for your journey is to take a good long look at the sky, watch the movement of clouds by day, and take in the immaculate view of our Universe on a clear night at every opportunity to help put things into perspective.

Homeostasis – A State Of Supreme Balance

The term *Homeostasis* was coined by Walter B Cannon (1871-1945) who was an American physiologist. He noted that our bodies have balancing mechanisms built in to counteract certain stresses. Each body structure, from the cellular to the systemic level, contributes in some way to keeping the internal environments of our bodies *within normal limits.*

Within our immaculate bodies there are two major recognised systems within our Autonomic Nervous System (ANS), which maintain balance in our responses. The ANS controls our bodily functions that are not consciously directed, including regular beating of the heart, intestinal movements, perspiration and salivation and also our responses to stress, our 'fight or flight' reflexes. The two sections are referred to as the Sympathetic System and the Parasympathetic System. The Sympathetic System reacts as a counter balance to trigger our responses to stress for survival. However, if we're under *continuous* stress our bodies are depleted of energy and we become in danger of falling ill, so that's why it's so valuable for us to find our *own* rules of balance.

As well as learning the enormous benefits of regular in-depth relaxation, it's important to be aware that we all need a *certain amount* of stress in our lives to be able to function properly and to help maintain our self-esteem. We just need to keep the balance. When we have balance and an understanding of our own needs and abilities, we find the key to our life. With this new approach instead of wasting enormous amounts of energy on things, which don't work for us in a positive way, we can free up our energies and send them in the right direction and even exceed our expectations ~ *keep me posted!*

As a natural therapist I strongly believe that *'prevention'* is the way forward in healthcare and I hope in the future we'll see more people attending to preventing illness and not waiting to become ill first before they make changes to their lifestyles. With the emphasis on 'healthy balance', *a good doctor/patient relationship is pure healing in motion!* With greater awareness there's so much more we can learn about the immaculate powers of healing the body, mind and spirit too.

It's important to also be aware that it's not only what we digest, but in addition, what we physically and mentally absorb that consequently we become, and that our living environment has an enormous affect on our health and well-being.

Taking 'real time out' from our lives however simple, and whatever our lifestyle, helps us to regain balance.

The medical professions now agree that at least 80% of illness is caused by and certainly aggravated by stress, (and indeed M.E./C.F.S. anxiety and depression have greatly been associated to long term stress) and the key to coping and recovery is finding the right balance.

Whilst we're in the process of healing ourselves and in addition to regular relaxation times, gentle exercise such as walking helps to reduce pent-up negative energy and naturally gives us a feeling of being re-charged. It can also help to encourage natural sleep patterns. This is good to know if you're studying because getting plenty of fresh air also refreshes the mind, makes us more alert and can enhance our memory.

Here are a few things to remember: *Simple to know but even better to remind ourselves of every so often!*

- With exercise, the right level of activity should leave you slightly breathless but not speechless.
- Treat yourself daily with nourishing foods.
- It's good to plan and have positive goals for yourself.
- The best time to tackle any administration work is after a good walk of about 15 to 20 minutes

when your mind is fresh and alert and stress
levels are reduced.
- Try to maintain hobbies or maybe seek out
  some new interests.
- It's good to keep your social life going and stay
  in contact with friends.
- Plan ahead for days out and arrange holidays
  away if possible so you have got things to look
  forward to.
- Keep boredom at bay by changing the subject
  as often as possible and keep a 'healthy mind,
  healthy body' attitude.
- Look at possibilities for change in your life.

*Whatever else we are investing in within our
lives; investing in our health is the most important
investment we can make.*

Maintain Homeostasis in your life

*It's sometimes as if people are constantly juggling while
trying to win some sort of race, life is not a race...if
it were then what happens when you reach the finish
line?*

Sadly you DO NOT win.

*Life can be short, so surely the essence should be to
savour every God given moment and to enjoy this truly
breathtakingly beautiful magnificent world of ours?*

11

Elizabeth Bailey

If it's at the cost of your life's energies to obtain as many riches as possible in the shortest time, then at least take real time out at each and every moment possible.

Many of us are spinning too fast through our lives. We have all the knowledge and capabilities to actually produce a Heaven on earth, and as we know life could be blissful if it weren't for man made poverty and greed – which we have the power to change.

Why is it that it's only when we go through enough traumas ourselves that we stop and wonder what life's all about?

It's 'there', that eventually we find our 'true' selves.

Through 'truth' we find the way.

Sacred Space

It's important to our mind, body and spiritual balance that we should all have our own 'sacred space' to be able to go where we can feel protected and at peace.

One of the most important things to remember, whatever our lifestyle, is to find regular times each day to relax, meditate or simply just take time to sit quietly. The practice of regular relaxation and meditation helps our nervous system to regulate balance and ultimately helps to bring about a state of inner peace. It is essential to help lessen physical and psychological stress and can help us to deal with our lives with a more focussed and positive approach.

Reminding ourselves to be still and 'at one' with ourselves is crucial to our health and well-being. By practicing regular relaxation we can still our mind (and it gets to really enjoy it!). We help to balance our blood pressure levels, slow our heartbeat and breathing down to a state of supreme rest and reduce the strain on our body as a whole.

Here are some suggestions for a lifetime that can help to avoid excess stress and distractions in your daily home environment: Try to: -

- Practice ignoring the telephone if you don't feel like answering it.
- Turn your mobile off, often.
- Don't feel you have to immediately answer text messages and give yourself a well-earned break.
- Try not to be 'available' to everyone at every moment, only to yourself.

The bedroom is an ideal place to have your own space to relax in or you can make your own space anywhere as long as it's special to you and kept that way. I find surrounding the area with tea light candles and crystals brings a calming influence. Even making your own version of an altar is a lovely idea. The important thing is that it's your *'own sacred space'* surrounded by the things you love (try not to include photographs of others in this space, keep them in another area of your room). Try to keep your sacred space only for you and you alone.

Tips for the Boudoir

It's good to keep your bedroom as your 'sanctuary' most of these suggestions should help to ease you into associating your bedroom specifically as a place of rest and sleep (highly recommended cuddles permitted of course!).

N

W   E

S

If possible make sure your headboard is in the North!

The magnetic pole forces of gravity on Earth can have an affect on sleep patterns and it's believed that sleeping with your head in the North gives a more restful sleep.

Natural crystals and their healing powers make a beautiful addition to any bedroom. Crystal tea light holders made from **quartz crystal** and **rose quartz** provide tranquil light so you have a combination of both crystal and *healing light* energies flowing around you. Crystal tea light holders are safe to use in the bedroom as you wind down to go to sleep. Of course, always extinguish the flame before you go to sleep and never leave a candle to burn unattended.

Small tumble stone natural crystals can have a great calming effect on sleep patterns when placed under your pillow or at your bedside. Ideal crystals for helping to induce sleep are **rose quartz, amethyst and clear quartz crystal.** There's more information about the benefits of natural crystals in a later chapter.

Sleep disturbance can affect anyone and our sleep can be directly disturbed if we are suffering from illness or stress. It is also estimated that at least 50% of us are suffering from some form or other of sleep depravation. Some tried and tested tips that I totally recommend to help ease this are: -

1. **Try to keep your telephone away from your bed.** Telephones have electromagnetic fields around them, as do computers. In fact electrical equipment like this should be kept away from the bedroom. If you have a telephone in your bedroom try to keep it 4-5 feet away from your head when resting, relaxing and most importantly when trying to sleep.

2. **If possible, remove the television from your bedroom.** Watching the television excites our brain waves and can be 'energy depleting' which is a vital factor in recovery, particularly from M.E./C.F.S. and when coping with anxiety. Try to remember to turn the television off when not in use. TV's which are left on standby emit electromagnetic waves which affect our brain wave patterns and can cause anxiety, depression and emotional changes, and bring on headaches and tension. (I told you this was about awareness – it's all productive news though!).

3. **Try not to have your mobile phone in the bedroom.** Mobiles emit potent electromagnetic fields, which can disturb brain waves. Of course

they do have their benefits in emergencies outside the bedroom!

4. **Make sure your room can be made as dark as possible.** Try to invest in some blackout curtains or blinds if you have any form of light beaming into your sanctuary. When we are in the dark it's a scientific fact that we release more of the wonderful hormone melatonin and are lulled off naturally and stay asleep until we are ready to spring into action the next day. *It will come! Our sleep patterns like everything else have ebbs and flows.*

It's a good idea to prepare your 'space' for doing your relaxation and meditations.

Always make sure the area is warm and comfortable and free from draughts and disturbance. You could also light a candle for yourself to symbolise peace and association with rest.

This book is all about changes but they're all good and I promise, with practice you'll find it hard to go back to your old ways once you've tried these.

Observe cats - they're the experts when it comes to relaxation!

A Guide to A Daily Routine

Try to follow daily patterns of ACTIVITY then REST.
As you progress with your recovery gradually increase
activity times and reduce rest times but always maintain
rest/meditation daily. It may appear that there's a lot
of resting at first but it's exactly what your body, mind
and soul needs just at the moment and as you get your
energy back and start to feel better you can adjust times
to suit your condition. This isn't only if you're suffering
from anxiety, depression, stress or M.E./C.F.S - it's for
everyone!

If you're working or have children simply adjust the
routine timing to suit your commitments, but ensure
that the same crucial principles of rest and relaxation
still apply.

Here's a rough guide to how your day could go.

- Start the day by listening to your favourite positive up beat music.
- Have a nutritious breakfast (try to include a piece of fresh fruit at breakfast time to boost your vitamin and mineral intake and energy levels).
- Try to shower and make an effort to look your best no matter how you're feeling, as it can help to improve your circulation and help to lift your spirits.
- Prepare your 'sacred space' and follow a relaxation exercise as suggested later.
- Return from your relaxation slowly and do an activity in the house, pacing yourself as you go, dividing chores up into small and manageable tasks with rest times in between.
- Choose an activity such as a short walk for 15 – 20 minutes.
- Do 15 minutes only of administration work you may need to do.
- Enjoy a healthy snack, fruit and drink about 11am.
- Do your rest and relaxation routine (see following chapter).
- Choose a light activity.
- Have a nutritious lunch like a salad, sushi, omelette, tomatoes on toast with grated cheese, jacket potato or fresh soups, followed by a dessert of yoghurt, fromage fraise, piece of fresh fruit or a chocolate mousse – "yes, go on

there's plenty of time to burn off the calories before dinner time!"

- Enjoy another rest time.
- Choose an activity like preparing the vegetables for the evening meal or work at the computer for a maximum of 30 minutes. Possibly find something interesting to research?
- Do a short session of gentle yoga or ballet exercises as described in a later chapter.
- Prepare and enjoy your evening meal.
- Enjoy another rest and relaxation time or sit quietly in meditation.
- Prepare for a minimum of 30 minutes wind down before bed (tips suggested in a further chapter).
- Be ready for sleep as soon as the light is out and look forward to a brand new day with new adventures and further progress tomorrow.

I promise you it 'is' possible to still get things done, as the saying goes, less haste, more speed!

Rest and Relaxation Times

The suggestions in this book for relaxation explore visualisation to help you begin to get in touch with your inner self and bring awareness to healing. Quietening the mind gives the whole body a rest. Learning to relax fully without any distractions and taking our brains thought patterns down to a minimum just after 15 minutes can relax and refresh us. In-depth relaxation is truly an art and when practiced regularly can also bring about experiences of deeper awareness and clarity of thought.

By balancing our nervous system through simple methods of regular relaxation and meditation our energies are replenished and the benefits can be felt as if having had up to four hours sleep.

My suggestion for survival of a lifetime is that you should take at least one day in seven to totally relax. Do no work, nor exercise, apart from flexing your feet up and down and stretching your arms out in front of you slowly clenching your fists a few times. Try to eat light nutritious meals and rest in whichever way you feel is your way to unwind.

The art of meditation and deep relaxation in the teachings of yoga has been practiced for centuries particularly in the Eastern part of the World. There was a wave of interest in the 1960's when it seemed to gain the label of the hippy sector. Today, thankfully, the physical and emotional benefits of practicing yoga and meditation are once again being re-discovered and, as it should be, without stigma, and it's effects are being recognised as a valuable way to achieving balance in our lives.

Being an enormous fan of relaxation and meditation I, however, hadn't practiced yoga for many years before falling victim to M.E./C.F.S. so it was my wake up call to start up again. Not having any relaxation tapes to hand, I made my own. Some people recommend changing relaxation routines for a variety but I found my own tape I learnt off by heart and could then do it in my mind almost anywhere at anytime. (Please visit my website for more information, contact details are on the *about the author* page at the back of this book).

Remember to stretch beautifully as much as you can when you wake up and after every relaxation. Stretch for as long as your body feels it wants to. It's a great feeling and tones all your muscles in one go by flattening, lengthening and refreshing them naturally with oxygenated blood.

Meditation and In-Depth Relaxation

(For clarity of thought, inner peace, total rest, better sleep, top up energy levels like never before, feelings of well being and younger looks!).

It's a medical fact that relaxation and meditation if practiced for a length of time reduces fatigue, nervousness, anxiety disorders, stress and relaxes our involuntary nervous system, as a whole, in the same way as full sleep, yet being in a state of consciousness. Don't let it deter you if you've previously not practiced in-depth relaxation, and at first you find it difficult to keep focussed. This happens to many an experienced meditator! It's the idea of disciplining the mind as well as the body that helps us to relax fully and deeply. There are lots different types of meditation techniques and it's just a case of trying them to see which one works best for you.

IT TAKES PRACTICE AND PERSEVERENCE TO CALM THE MIND. If you haven't practiced in depth-relaxation or meditation before, usually within about 7 days you'll have trained your mind to wind down. It's an extremely powerful organ of ours!

Through getting into the practice of relaxation, meditation and taking time out to simply 'be', it's possible that you can eventually reach a point where pure healing takes place and you begin to see your own life as an observer. You can then begin to see what changes need to be made. This can bring a whole new dimension to your awareness and can be a truly enriching experience.

A simple yet powerful technique of 'body scanning' is extremely beneficial for in-depth relaxation and can either be done on a soft mat on the floor or on a bed and can be modified to a sitting position, so can even be done while you're on a train or bus journey!

To prepare for relaxation make sure the room is warm and that you won't be disturbed in any way.

If possible lie completely flat on your bed without a pillow. This may take a little practice, but gradually work towards this for maximum benefit by reducing the amount of pillow support you give to your head (if you have high blood pressure have a small pillow to support your head and neck).

In deep relaxation the breath becomes slower and your body begins to lose heat so it's important to cover yourself lightly with a blanket. Fleece blankets are light, warm and ideal for this.

You may find that you feel like sighing or yawning whilst you are doing your relaxation programme, which is a good sign. It's just your body relaxing into what it's supposed to be doing.

Relaxation Exercise

It's good to have a drink of water prepared near by prior to your relaxation. Drinking water after your relaxation can help to both detoxify and refresh you.

This position is called the 'Corpse Pose' in yoga practice and although it's name sounds a bit gruesome, it's the most regenerative yoga posture there is!

Make sure you wear loose, light, warm clothing with no restrictions, particularly around the waistline area, and ladies, undo your bra or better still take it off.

It's always a good idea to wear a pair of socks to keep your feet extra warm. If you're lying down make sure you lie in a straight position so that your spine is straight and that your chin is slightly tucked in.

Have a little more than hip width distance between your feet and just relax your legs so your feet are flopped out to each side. Have your arms about 12 inches away from your body each side with the palms of your hands facing upward and let your fingers just curl naturally.

If comfortable, it's best to breathe through your nose throughout the relaxation, air breathed in is purified by tiny hairs in your nostrils and warmed to the perfect temperature for your lungs this way.

So now you have yourself lying on the bed or floor and you have covered yourself lightly with a blanket, it's time to relax for 20 minutes. You may have other thoughts come into your head but try to imagine those thoughts just for this moment in time disappearing on a cloud. You can deal with those thoughts some other time. Just for this moment in time you are relaxing and recharging your energies.

First gently close your eyes and keep them closed until I suggest that you open them again.

When our eyes are closed it cuts out distractions helping to calm the mind. It's naturally restful and helps us to look within.

Listen out for any sounds that you can hear outside the room and be aware of those sounds, life is going on around you but just for this moment in time you are completely relaxing. Then take your attention to any sounds you may hear in the room.

Bring your awareness to the feeling of all of your weight being fully supported by the bed or chair beneath you.

Now bring your attention right down to your toes, be aware of your toes and imagine that they are warm and relaxed.

Bring your attention to the soles of your feet, feel that they are soft and warm and at rest.

Be aware of your ankles, feel that the area of your ankles is relaxed and that your feet are feeling heavy and sinking into the bed.

Travel within your mind to the backs of your calves. Feel that they are soft and relaxed.

Allow the backs of your knees to relax. Be aware of your thighs, soft and heavy as if melting into the bed. Feel the whole of your legs becoming very, heavy sinking deep into the bed.

Bring your attention to the area of your buttocks. Feel the area soft and relaxed. Feel your pelvis sinking right back, deep into the bed.

Now bring your attention to the area around your waist. Feel that it is freely moving with a gentle flow of movement with no restriction. Feel the gentle rise of your abdomen with each breath you take.

Now feel your back flat and wide against the bed and imagine that your shoulders are peeling right back as if melting into the bed, leaving the whole of your chest area open with the freedom of your breath.

Take a deep slow breath in to expand your lungs and on the inhalation imagine that you are *breathing in new life and new energy.* Pause with that breath for a second then release all of the breath in a sigh and *imagine that you are breathing away and letting go of any tiredness and tension.* Just let go.

Take your attention now to the tops of your arms; feel that they are soft, warm and relaxed.

Your elbows are gently relaxed and just for this moment in time they are motionless and resting perfectly aligned.

Feel that your forearms are limp and heavy, sinking into the bed.

The palms of your hands are warm and soft and your fingers are curled naturally.

Now bring your attention back up your arm slowly to the area of your armpits, feel this area is soft and relaxed.

Bring your attention to your neck area, feel that your neck is smooth and relaxed and just to release any tension very slowly, *as if in slow motion,* turn your head to the right and back to the centre, then over to the left and back to the centre.

Now pay special attention to your lower jaw, make sure that you aren't clenching any of your teeth and that your tongue is lying relaxed in your mouth.

Think of your mouth and lips being in a perfect state of softness.

Picture your cheeks soft, warm and glowing with health.

Imagine that your eyes have been kissed closed.

Your temples are soft, cool, relaxed and free of any pressure, your eyebrows are restful.

Travel with your attention to the point at the back of your head where your head makes contact with the bed or pillow. Now feel all of your hair relaxing and falling right back in that direction.

Enjoy the feeling of gravity, feel the bed supporting you, sinking into it and letting go, knowing that you are perfectly safe and supported by the bed.

Imagine your hair growing thick and healthy.

And picture every cell in your body being re-energised and every organ being rested and refreshed.

Feel your whole self now to be very soft, very heavy, very relaxed and sinking into the bed.

Imagine yourself for a moment floating on a cloud away from any concerns. Life is going on around you but you are now totally relaxed and re-charging your energies.

Simply enjoy the total peace and tranquillity of the moment.

Now travel in your mind to the area just below your chest right in the centre of your being, known as the solar plexus, where all of your nerves and energies meet together and imagine a bright golden light glowing from this area like a bright candle flame. It's glowing gently and filling your whole body with wave after wave of brilliant golden light. This light being so bright that it reaches every part of your being and glows beyond your body.

Feel the complete peace and tranquillity of the moment. Ask yourself within to be reminded of this wonderful peace and gentleness and remember this feeling is *always within your reach.* (Make sure your eyelids are still softly closed)

Now to bring yourself back from the relaxation, still keep your eyes closed and first take your awareness to your breath and notice it's gentle ebb and flow, enjoy this awareness for a moment then gradually make your breath a little stronger and deeper.

Now bring your attention back to your toes and fingers and start to wriggle them gently back and forth, then your hands and feet, then gradually *without any strain* take really deep long luxurious stretches. Stretch your whole body in any direction you want it to stretch. Try not to overstretch, just go with the flow. Stretch and yawn fully, the more you screw up your face in a yawn the more refreshed and relaxed your facial muscles will be reducing the appearance of tiredness and tension.

Then gently bend your knees and roll over onto your *right* side (this helps to free the main artery to distribute oxygenated blood around your body).

As you progress with your recovery try to stay awake through relaxation exercises to help you balance your nightly sleep patterns. As you come back from the relaxation, before opening your eyes, affirm to yourself in your mind that when you get up you'll feel refreshed and relaxed and ready to continue with the rest of your day.

Gently return from the relaxation by slowly opening your eyes and take a few moments to focus. Very slowly, as if in slow motion again, bring yourself up to a seated position. Take as long as you need, then gradually stand up and gently ease yourself back into your day.

A Healing Relaxation

Relaxation Exercise

This is a particularly good method of relaxation combined with a beautiful visualisation using the suggestion of a healing colour, again focussing on the visualisation of glowing and surrounding.

Once again using all the preparation as previously suggested: -

(Remembering if any thoughts do come into your mind practice just watching them float away as if on a cloud, what's important is the here and now)

Make sure you aren't going to be disturbed in any way and get yourself comfortable on the bed or floor preferably and cover yourself with a light warm blanket, not forgetting that those important toes of yours need extra warmth too.

Keeping your spine straight but relaxed when you are lying flat with your arms and legs stretched out, as suggested, is an important factor when relaxing. It enables the spine, with its thousands of nerve impulses to relax as much as possible. A simple way to check that your spine is aligned and that your back is flat against the floor: -

Place your hands as if in a prayer position, gently resting your hands on your breastbone. Then keeping your palms together point your fingers forward, and without strain, stretch your arms out in front of you at shoulder height for a second or two. Then gently place them back on the floor about 12 inches away from your sides, palms facing upward in the resting position. Again with the feet out as before have a little wriggle until you *feel* it feels right. It's important to feel comfortable, but make sure you keep your spine in a straight line.

Gently close your eyes to give you the chance to calm your mind.

Take three breaths in deeply filling your lungs *without strain* just until it feels comfortable and imagine breathing *in new energy, wisdom and health*, pause just for a second then let all that breath go with a *sigh and imagine breathing out any negative thoughts and energy blockages* - leaving your body open and free to relax.

Feel your body is supported by the floor; knowing that you are completely safe with the Earth underneath you through your bed and the floor, into the ground through the rocks and into the core of the Earth's energies, you are safe and cradled.

Feel that your body is soft and limp as if it's melting into the bed.

Imagine your whole body now from the crown of your head to the tips of your toes being surrounded by a clear sapphire blue bright healing light which glows around you, bringing healing to your body, mind and spirit. The healing colour of sapphire blue is nurturing your body physically, mentally and emotionally. Feel that every cell and organ in your body is being renewed with healthy cells. Feel that you are at one with yourself and in tune to your body as a whole and healing your mind, body and spirit uniting them to heal.

Stay with that feeling and bring your attention to your feet, and scanning your body again feel that they are heavy and soft, feel your ankles are limp and relaxed.

Feel that your feet and legs are softly relaxed, letting go of any tension; imagine it melting away into the floor.

Picture your abdomen and chest soft and at ease with a gentle movement to that area.

Your chest area is open, giving you freedom of breath.

Feel that your throat area is relaxed and clear giving you the freedom of speech.

Your face is relaxed and glowing with the radiance of health.

Picture your whole body is being bathed in a beautiful sapphire blue light, healing every cell and nerve along the way.

With each breath you take imagine that as you inhale you are breathing in a bright white light from the top of your head through your crown chakra (energy centre). As you exhale, feel the light flowing right down through your body and returning to the Earth through your feet and washing away any negative thoughts with it. It returns to the Earth where any negative energy is safely exchanged into positive energy. Do this three times to enhance your energy flow.

Now imagine yourself being surrounded further within a golden bubble of healing light for protection.

Your whole body now is totally relaxed and receptive to the healing colour and you are at one.

Savour this feeling for a few moments and if your mind begins to wonder bring your thoughts back, take three deep breaths in and out and again visualise the beautiful healing lights.

To bring yourself back from the healing relaxation be aware first of your breath and very gradually, without strain make it a little stronger, then start to wriggle your fingers and toes.

Bring your awareness back into your room hearing all the sounds that go on around you and being aware of your surroundings.

Elizabeth Bailey

*To refresh your eyes gently stroke your eyelids from the nose outward three times stroking from the bottom of your lid outward then the middle then the eye socket area.

Have an enormous stretch for as long as you feel you want to without strain. Stretch your whole body in whichever direction it's asking you to stretch and when you are ready, gently bend your knees and roll over onto your *right* side.

Lie there for a few moments and when you feel ready, as if in slow motion again, bring yourself up to a seated position, feeling refreshed and relaxed and ready to carry on with whatever the day has in store for you. Carry the feeling of a relaxed and open mind with you throughout your day.

If you can practice these exercises every day and perhaps my other guided meditation, you'll be well on the way to enjoying not only physical, but also spiritual well being in a profound way.

Happy relaxing!

This is a beautiful affirmation passed on to me by my yoga instructor I want to share with you. It sums up where we get to in meditation and can bring Heavenly awareness to humanity.

Namaste

I honour the place in you
In which the entire Universe dwells

I honour a place in you
Which is of Love, of Truth, of Light
And of Peace

When you are in that place in you
And I am in that place in me
We are one

GHANDI

Blissful Sleep

It's only when we are asleep that growth and repair takes place in our bodies - a crucial time for recuperation and healing.

When we approach time to go to sleep at night and as it becomes darker outside, our bodies begin to produce more of the hormone *melatonin*. This hormone is produced by the Pineal gland deep within our brains and prepares us for sleep, which gives us the feelings of tiredness and relaxation. Also the human growth hormone is produced whilst we are in the blissfully regenerative state of sleep.

People who suffer from blindness do not naturally produce melatonin. As they have no light perception, their nerve impulses simply don't differentiate between dark and light, therefore many blind people need to take a melatonin supplement to induce sleep. When our primitive brain tells us to sleep it's crucial that we do, to enable us to function with balance in our lives.

Agricultural lifestyles are really what our primitive nature thrives on, going to bed early when it starts to get dark and getting up with the lark at dawn!

At dawn our eyes react to the light and this stimulates us to wake up. If our bodies are rested enough we wake up naturally, *bliss*.

It's interesting to remember that our thought and behavioural patterns can be adversely affected by even just 10% lack of sleep.

Sleep deprivation affects everyone to some extent and we know that adequate sleep and rest times make us feel better and it's important to get enough exercise too. By exercising this in turn can give us a better quality of sleep and the body, mind and spirit as a whole can then return to its natural balanced state once fully rested.

It's a fact that we function better mentally during the first four hours of waking, so this is an ideal time to tackle administration.

Clearing Down

A great way to clear down negative thought patterns before sleep and indeed, at anytime, is to allow yourself to imagine when breathing in through your nose and deep into your lungs that your whole body is being showered from above by a bright silvery white light. Picture this light covering every part of you bringing with it positive energy to every cell in your body. As you exhale, picture any negative thoughts and stale energy being released down through your feet into the ground and out through your breath as a dull grey mist. Repeat this exercise three times.

Winding Down Before Bedtime

When coping with stress or illness it's 'particularly' important to allow time to wind down before sleep. Try to wind down for at least half an hour before you go to sleep. It's a lovely way to end each day, to reflect, and importantly, to think positively and it can greatly assist regular sleep patterns and help towards having a better quality of sleep.

Winding down suggestions:

- **Enjoy a warm bath and surround it with a few tea lights***:* Turn the light off and relax and soak away, this will leave you feeling cosy, warm and relaxed. Bathing also helps to dilate blood vessels and can help to promote better circulation so it can be most beneficial particularly if suffering from M.E./C.F.S., stress, anxiety and depression. Sounds simple, but it works!

- **Have a warm, preferably milky, drink or a herbal tea** (without any caffeine) half an hour before you turn your light out. It's a fact that the lactose in milk helps us to produce more of the gorgeous sleep-inducing hormone melatonin, which helps our bodies to synchronise our 24-hour internal clocks. There is special night-time milk available at supermarkets now, which comes from cows milked later in the day! Their milk contains more of the hormone melatonin. This wonderful natural hormone naturally slows the heart rate and reduces alertness, readying the body for sleep. Regular drinking of the night-time milk is reported to help improve sleep patterns within weeks. There are also some delicious herbal teas which you could try, and many of them can have calming effects. Try to avoid peppermint tea in the evenings, because as the word suggests, it peps you up, so do citrus flavoured teas, but they're all fantastic for the mornings!

- **Take a hot water bottle with you to bed.** Warmth helps to unblock pain at cellular level and induces relaxation. For best results wrap the hot water bottle up and enjoy a good cuddle!

- **Try to avoid reading just before sleep.** Scientifically proven, reading takes up a lot of energy and excites our thought patterns too much before sleep.

- **Use this lovely YOU time to simply reflect 'positively' on your day.** Don't try and solve all your problems. If negative thoughts do come into your head counter-balance them and think *positively* that you will give them thought at *another time*. This may take practice, but practice makes perfect!

- **This is 'your' time to give 'yourself' the essential rest you need.** To be stronger in mind, body and soul and to be able to deal with things everyday.

- **It's a great idea to do one of the relaxation techniques from this programme or similar.** Just before your half hour wind down time, but still try to have 30 minutes to wind down before sleep. It gets your thought waves quietened down and prepares you for the sleep ahead. As the quality of your sleep improves and you progress, gradually reduce your wind down time, but never ever give it up, even if it's just for 10 minutes.

- **Last but by no means least, try to count your blessings at the end of each day**. Giving thanks to the Universe brings positive energy back. Something magical happens when we are grateful. It brings positive and happy energies back to us in return.

Ways to soothe your mind, body and soul before falling asleep

- *Enjoy a healing sensation*: We all have the ability to heal others and ourselves. A lovely soothing way to calm the mind, as you close your eyes to go to sleep, is to rest your hand on your solar plexus area (the upper belly), take a slow deep breath in through your nose and out through your mouth for three breaths, then return your breath to a normal breathing pattern. Bring your attention to the gentle rise and fall of your abdomen as you breathe and focus your mind on nothing else except your healing breath and the warmth of your hand.

We all have an aura of energy around us consisting of heat and vibration, which can be felt and seen. Many people claim that they can see auras, which can appear as different colours according to one's state of health.

Awareness of auras surrounding life form has been known for thousands of years and interest in this is becoming popular again, particularly as auras can now be seen scientifically by the incredible method of Aura photography.

- *Aura Smoothing* is a lovely method, which helps to clear the mind at the end of the day, and smooth out negative energy helping you offload your worries or concerns before sleep:

Starting from your head, work with the palms of your hands flat but relaxed. Work downward from the crown of your head (about an inch away from your body) also include smoothing each arm on the top and underneath and flick off negative energy at the ends. Simply work down your body as far as comfortable. You can do the back of your head and body too but only do what feels comfortable for you **without strain**. Repeat from the top of your head to the magical power of three times to help to let go of any tension.

- *Stress-less sleep:* Occasionally using a tiny bit of pure *essential oil of lavender* on a tissue near your bed can be helpful if you ever feel stressed. I also find that ***Dr Edward Bach's flower essence remedies*** and particularly, ***Rescue Remedy*** drops can be beneficial for stressful times, also the odd 2-3 day dose at the beginning of a recovery programme can be of help giving comfort and reassurance. The drops can be taken in water or on the tongue. They can be just as effective if placed on your pulse points on your wrists or gently massaged onto each of your temples. (Contact details for the Dr Edward Bach centre just in case you haven't heard of this wonderful man are included in the back pages of this book).

After about the first week of starting your new routine try go to bed and get up at a regular time. Our bodies love healthy routines and can respond beautifully!

- If you find yourself unable to get off to sleep or waking in the night with your mind racing, a really effective way of releasing your thoughts is to keep a notebook by your bedside and write down your thoughts as they come. *Don't hold back!* If you're angry or worried, use whatever words you feel you need to be able to *release* and let go of how you're feeling. If you're feeling happy it's just as beneficial to record your thoughts in a positive way. Destroy any negative notes in the morning but keep hold of the good ones.

Try and get at least the recommended 8 (minimum 7) hours sleep and preferably 9. Don't worry if you're not able to sleep for the whole time, *resting* your body is important too. Our sleep patterns affect us all as individuals. I suggest simply do what feels right for *you* and consult your doctor if you have any particular concerns regarding any persistent problems with your sleep patterns.

Our sleep patterns can be greatly improved when we work towards balance in our lives through regular rest, exercise, stimulation and eating patterns.

Sweet dreams!

The Benefits of Exercise

Our lives and the Universe are full of immaculate natural energies down to every last molecule - a spark of energy causes our hearts to beat...

(Always check with your doctor first before commencing any exercise routine if you have any particular concerns about your health).

It's important to approach and maintain a very gradual introduction and build up to exercise, some people diagnosed with M.E./C.F.S. join gyms to get fitter with disastrous results. I can't emphasise enough the need to be controlled and listen to your body at every level of this programme of exercise. In contrast, however, if you're suffering from stress the gym could be a very good place for you to investigate, but it's all a matter of personal choice. One thing for sure is that if it's possible we all need to keep *mobile,* particularly when we've been immobile for a time.

The fantastic benefits of exercise are so important to our well-being both physically and mentally.

I've listed a few of the routines, I suggest you try because they can help enormously to get on the road to recovery, build strength in your muscles and nervous system and if maintained, can also keep your body nicely toned with surprisingly little effort!

The Facts:

Exercise: - Re-oxygenates all living cells of your body.

Encourages and assists peristalsis: (the involuntary movement of food inside us) and helps to get rid of waste matter regularly – which we all know is a very important fact of life!

Exercise helps to build bone density: The impact of the movement of *gentle* weight bearing during exercise helps our bones, whatever their age, to strengthen and repair. Our bones are full of living cells inside and out, and with stimulus, their cell production increases and they become even stronger. Along with a good supply of calcium, it's possible to strengthen bones with exercise such as gentle walking, in fact the gentler it is, the better it is for us.

Exercise increases production of Synovial Fluid in our joints: This is a wonderful lubricating fluid that helps ease movement. It gradually increases the more we use our joints.

Exercise enables our lymphatic system to move and cleanses us of old or dead cells and viruses: This amazing network, which runs almost parallel to our circulatory system, is stimulated when we move our muscles by shifting debris; hence, if we get swollen glands, it's a sign that the battle has commenced! In yoga practice it's sometimes encouraged that the glands are gently smoothed out with hand movements to help dispel viruses. I won't be suggesting 'that' just at this time, but gentle exercise absolutely yes!

Exercise done in moderation, particularly walking, helps to regulate blood pressure.

Exercise also increases the release of the hormone serotonin, nature's anti-depressant: It's estimated that within just 15 minutes of walking, our bodies production of serotonin increases.

You are as healthy as your spine: By looking after your spine your whole body will benefit. The network of our nervous system runs through our spine a bit like an electric cable and is also very similar in that it carries energy and electrical impulses. Gently keeping the spine mobile brings fresh oxygenated blood to the area and therefore, helps to maintain a healthy balance of our nervous system supplying us with renewed energy. (See gentle Spinal Twist a little further on).

Always try to sit with your spine straight as much as possible *but keep your shoulders relaxed. This keeps the spine healthy, improves energy flow to all your organs and can help to tone up your tummy with the least of effort!*

Suggested Exercises

I suggest that for the first few days of your recovery programme and depending on your condition, only do physiotherapy work to gradually introduce your body to movement. Gentle walking can then be introduced which in itself is an ideal form of all-round exercise.

At a slow pace, take your first walk of the programme. I suggest if you feel OK, no more than 50 yards at first and then return home and rest. However, if you're trying to cope with depression, anxiety and stress and not suffering from M.E/C.F.S. or fatigue, walking is excellent for de-stressing so you can walk further but still maintain rest and relaxation times and pace yourself.

With regard to walking, try to increase walk times by only a few minutes in the second week but only increase very gradually and keep at a slow pace to maintain energy levels and to avoid any exertion.

Gradually build on the duration and length of your walks and don't push yourself beyond your comfortable limits, particularly during the first 2/3 months of your recovery. If you feel too tired, don't do your walk that day, you can always try again following day. As you recover, you'll be able to judge for yourself what goal you're aiming for, but it's important that you take everything in small stages.

As well as walking, yoga is a fantastic overall method of exercise as it brings about strength, awareness and balance of mind, body and spirit. It can help keep you supple and is for all ages, as postures can be greatly modified. You can build up strength very gradually with yoga practice. If you find a class to join, simply keep your teacher informed of your health and modify asanas (exercise movements). Finding the right teacher that suits you is the key. Professional instructors should be able to assist with anyone. There's no reason why anyone shouldn't be able to enjoy yoga.

It's a good idea to try to use your staircase and steps at home to build up strength in your leg muscles. We're certainly not going for step aerobics here! Just gentle easy steps. Gradually increase the amount you do as you progress. At first, just take three or four steps up and down. If you're fairly agile you could then try taking two steps up the stairs at a time. Start by holding on to the handrail and build up to not using the handrail at all, just pure muscle power!

Every step you take is one more towards your recovery.

During the second stage, (your body will tell you when it's ready to commence the second stage) gradually introduce slightly longer walks. I suggest you introduce these gradually to combat the possibility of a build up of lactic acid in your blood. I suggest you aim to walk every other day and try other gentle exercise on the remaining days, then rest totally on the 7th day.

There'll be plenty of time ahead when you're stronger to increase this and to adjust your life to suit your metabolism.

My ideas are guided suggestions and you'll need to read your own body to judge what you need. When you get into your routines you'll know when you start to feel better and how much you will want to increase your exercise routines according to your lifestyle. Don't give up, even when you do begin to feel better and always try to incorporate some exercise movement into your day.

If you do have a day when you're feeling you have lots more energy try to keep it contained! We've all done it, tried to cram everything we can in when we have the energy, only to feel wiped out the following day. This can be avoided by simply pacing yourself and maintaining balance. Increase gradually, remembering that you are all the time building on your energy reserves and your body will reward you for this in the coming weeks and months.

There's no 'time limit' to healing.

Whatever type of exercise you enjoy, whilst you're healing and recovering, I recommend a combination of very subtle yoga and physiotherapy exercises and suggest as follows:

- Walking on the spot with your bare feet, if possible on a soft cushion or mat. The aid of a cushion helps to increase the stimulation of the leg muscles.

- Complete any of the following exercises listed here (instructions will follow).
  Warm Up Exercise No. 1
  Warm Up Exercise No. 2
  Leg and Arm Stretches
  Gentle Spinal Twist
  Chest Expander Exercise

Warm Up Exercise No. 1 (combining yoga and physiotherapy)

Lie on a bed and place your hands at your side palms downward, keeping your knees straight. Slowly lift your right leg up and down and take it only as far as you can without straining. Repeat with your right leg. Continue three times with each leg.

Bring your knees up towards your chest keeping your shoulders flat on the bed. Slowly and without strain take your knees just a couple of inches to each side alternately. Then bring them back to the centre and gently hug them into your chest to rest.

Warm Up Number 2 (or an exercise in itself)

In a standing position with your feet placed about 6 inches apart to help you balance, stand tall as if you are being pulled upwards, like a puppet, by an imaginary piece of string and keep your chest area relaxed.

Follow with walking movements on the spot for six paces each side, preferably on a cushion to tone the muscles.

If balancing proves to be difficult this exercise can also be performed whilst lying on a soft mat, or whilst sitting in a chair (try to make sure you're keeping your spine straight).

Standing or sitting tall once more try to get your balance by feeling your feet placed firmly flat on the floor.

Moving your balance onto your right foot, keeping your knees straight, lift your heel a few inches from the floor and flex your foot and toes forward and back. Do this three times each side, staying balanced. Repeat with your other foot. Then rotate each ankle first clockwise three times, and then anticlockwise three times. Finally, gently shake out any tension in your legs.

Slowly and gradually increase the repetition of these movements as you progress with your recovery.

Elizabeth Bailey

Leg and Arm Stretches

To help keep your circulation going and prevent stiffness in your joints when you have a day of rest, simple leg stretches can be done on your bed.

Whilst lying down flat and keeping your heels flat on the bed, bend and flex both feet up and down three times each pointing your toes downward and upward as you go.

(As time progresses and you improve, try to gradually lift your feet and legs slightly higher, about 2 inches off the bed).

* * *

In a seated position, stretch your arms straight out, palms facing downwards in front of you at shoulder height. Support the outstretched arm at first by holding at the elbow with your other hand.

Slowly clench your fists, simultaneously curling your thumbs in first. Do this three times but if you experience any tension just stop. Shake out the tension gently and repeat the exercise if it's comfortable to do so with the other arm.

Gently shake out any tension afterwards and rotate your shoulder joints by bending your elbows out to the sides and draw very small circles with your elbows in the air, first clockwise then anticlockwise.

If comfortable, lie on your back and gently hug your knees to your chest in resting pose or gently on your side for a while to rest.

Gentle Spinal Twist

On waking up in the morning, every other day, to warm your muscles up as you lie flat, do a few foot stretches and arm stretches as mentioned previously. As long as you don't have any back problems you can do a very gentle version of a <u>Spinal Twist</u>. This is a wonderful movement for toning the nervous system and brings suppleness to your spine and is also fantastic for toning up your waistline!

* Lay on your back with your feet about a hip width apart. Bend your knees and put your arms down by each side with your palms facing downward, keeping your shoulders completely flat on the floor.

* As slowly as possible, let your knees lead the way and gently lean them very slightly without strain over to your right side. Only go a few inches at first to a position as far as is comfortable. Then take them back to the central position. Pause a moment. Then gently repeat the same movement to your left side and then again back to the centre. Try to do this movement three times to each side. If you're fairly supple, you can gently roll your head

to the opposite direction from the way you're tipping your knees.

* Slowly bring both knees up towards your chest and hug them and gently rock yourself in this position a little from side to side, this is known as the 'embryo pose' and can help to relieve tension in your lower back.

In yoga postures all of the muscles of the body are gently but powerfully worked. Unlike concentrating on just one group of muscles in other exercise routines, you gain overall strength, suppleness and all-important balance with the practice of yoga.

Chest Expander Exercise

This exercise is also fantastic for helping to beat depression:

We often sit with our shoulders slightly hunched without knowing it. This exercise is good for anyone, particularly if working at a desk most of the day. It can also be beneficial to do if you suffer from asthma.

Whilst doing yoga exercises it's beneficial to try to keep with fairly deep breathing and whilst holding postures, to keep with your own natural rhythm of breath. For instance, before commencing any movement inhale deeply through your nose and when you bend or move into a stretching position exhale. However, this is not vital, particularly when just starting to do yogic movements.

It's more important that you feel comfortable and move into postures without any strain.

A fantastic way to start the day and uplift and release energy is to do this yoga exercise which helps to open up your heart and chest area encouraging energy in the heart chakra (energy centre).

- Stand tall with your palms together at breastbone height as in a prayer position. Bring your awareness to the feeling of warmth radiating from your thumbs against your chest. Close your eyes and take a few deep breaths in and out through your nose.

- On an inhalation, keeping the palms of your hands together, at shoulder height, slowly push your palms forward to arms length (open your eyes if you prefer at this point).

- Turn your palms to face outward with the backs of your hands together and on your exhalation slowly and gently sweep your arms down (similar to as if doing the 'breast stroke' in swimming) so that they reach down to hip level and clasp your fingers together *without strain* behind your back (palms facing upward).
- On your next inhalation, stand tall and very gently raise your clasped hands together a little way, about 6-7 inches, **without strain.** Only go to where it feels comfortable. Hold this

position for a moment or two and take a few
natural breaths in that pose.

- Gradually reverse the movements by bringing
  your arms back slowly so that your palms meet
  again at arms length in front of you. Bring
  your hands back into prayer position at chest
  level and imagine the Earth's energies rising up
  through your feet and reaching every area of
  your being.

*Finally, bring your consciousness back into the here
and now, ready to continue with the rest of your day
feeling refreshed and re-energised.*

Ballet Bar Movements and Yoga Tips

Ballet bar work is wonderful for toning and strengthening
muscles. This is a great alternative to the daily
physiotherapy based exercises mentioned earlier.

You don't need to do these exercises daily, a little and
often is better.

- Stand tall as mentioned before. If you can use
  the back of a hard table chair to help to balance
  you. Lightly hold the back of the chair at your
  side. It should be just under an arm's length
  away (this position comes from holding your
  partner's hand in dance which I think is quite
  lovely!).

- Now do a few walking on the spot paces making sure you *feel* the movement, peel your feet back and forth off and onto the floor, not letting your toes actually leave the floor completely (like an exaggerated walk five times to warm up).

- With your knees straight, place your feet together then fan the ends of your feet out to each side **without any strain**. Your feet should now be in a 'V' shape. This is called the 'First Position' of the feet in ballet and is alone excellent for toning your leg muscles. Simple, subtle, but powerful stuff!

- Standing tall in this position:

   (Now *this* is the bit that will hopefully give you nicely toned ballerina buttocks, now *there's* a new nickname ~ with a bit of luck anyway!)

- Cup your hands gently at hip height in front of you with your fingertips only just touching (elbows gently bent).

- Now squeeze your buttocks in tight and hold for five seconds, then release.

Do this three times every other day.

The last part of this exercise can even be practiced when waiting at the supermarket checkout. It's great to ease the boredom and also helps you work towards something positive!

Cerebral Stimulation

Don't forget to Exercise your Brain
Healthy mind – healthy body!

- Doing crossword puzzles can have a great stimulating effect on the brain. By using memory recall we are stimulating our short and long- term memory, just doing the easy crosswords in the newspaper daily can help keep your memory sharper. *Try it and see.*

- Try to get some balls! The art of juggling is excellent for helping to stimulate and keep the brain and reflex system alert sharpening the mind and challenging the 'brain fog' that comes with M.E./C.F.S., depression, anxiety and stress. Using both sides of our brain helps us to keep our brain sharp and our responses quicker. Try to keep practicing with your juggling balls ~ even a couple of oranges will do!

- Use both your left and right hand to do anything to keep both sides of your brain stimulated.

- Try board games like 'draughts' at first, then, as you feel better, 'chess' is great for stimulating the memory.

- Pretend you're an actor! The practice of learning lines in a play can help you to remember lots of other things. Learning and practicing just a few lines from your favourite films can be great fun to use or try a nice 'positive' poem. Then move on to new ones for even more memory recall stimulation.

Remember to use it ~ or lose it!

Exercise for the Brain

This is a great exercise for the neck and the shoulders. It helps to stimulate cerebral circulation and to clear 'brain fog'.

Standing tall or sitting with your back straight, slowly and gently turn your head to the right, then back to the centre, then to the left and back to the centre. Take your head downwards with your chin resting on your upper chest and back to the centre. Tilt your neck back very slowly, without strain, and back to the centre again.

For the shoulders: Gently cup your hands in front of you at tummy button level, having your elbows slightly bent. Pause, then, keeping your elbows slightly bent, lift your arms up in front of you and gracefully right up above your head. Pause.

Very slowly lower your arms out to each side in a wide circular motion at elbow height each side and then take them back to the centre again. Finally take them down into resting position at hip height in front of you, like a beautiful prima ballerina – male or female! Repeat this three times and increase to five times as you progress.

Crocodile Pose

One very simple, gentle and effective yoga pose is called the **'Crocodile Pose'.** It helps to stimulate and balance the neurological system, so it's perfect for M.E./C.F.S. stress, anxiety and depression.

This exercise should be avoided if you suffer from neck, back or joint problems.

- Try if you can to lay down with your tummy on the bed or a mat on the floor, with your feet together.

- Place your hands at ear-level with your arms outstretched in front of you, palms facing the floor. Keeping your chin down on the floor. Then gently bending your elbows bring your arms back towards you and lift your head slightly so that you can then rest your forehead on the backs of your hands.

- After a few seconds, keeping your elbows fairly wide, see if you can bring your elbows up and cup your chin in your hands, facing forwards in a resting position. Rest in that pose for a moment or two.

- You may remember doing this as a child whilst watching TV! If it feels comfortable, whilst you're still in this position, slowly bend your knees up and very gently swing your feet back and forth to exercise your leg muscles.

- Come out of the pose by slowly reversing your movements and by rolling back if possible (without strain) onto your knees and curl over so that your chest is lying on top of your thighs for a moment or two to counter-balance your posture. Place your arms loosely down by your sides (palms upward). This resting pose is called *'pose of a child'*. Gently curl back up again to finish. Alternatively, from your front lying position roll over onto your side for a moment or two with your knees bent slightly and slowly bring yourself up to a seated position.

We forget how to do this as we get older but it's a great way of stretching out our necks and stimulating our brains. You can work on gradually building up this posture working towards having your elbows bent fully and supporting your chin but never strain - remember if it doesn't feel comfortable don't do it.

Feel the Rhythm of Life – Dance!

- Another fantastic form of exercise is dancing. It's a great all round form of exercise and can affect our mood greatly.

- Dancing to a favourite piece of music with a bit of rhythm in it can be a wonderful cardio vascular workout at our own pace. Also the therapeutic swaying movement of dance soothes the body as a whole to cellular level!

- In Australia they have a wonderful holistic therapy widely used called 'pulsing' this is gentle rocking movements applied to the body all over, which can induce a beautifully calming, and healing effect. It can be likened to when we're on a smooth train journey in a gently rocking carriage and as infants being cradled and rocked in our carer's arms - dance has the same therapeutic rocking motion.

We are all full of energies, we are a mass of living buzzing cells, we are full of life's energy!

Food Glorious Food —
Ways to improve your Nutrition

Certain illnesses and conditions can be eased and even avoided when we learn to intelligently nourish ourselves.

I wrote *'Sacred Space'* with the intention to go back to research, discover and learn again the ability to minimise any strain on the body as a whole. Eating regularly is one of my main concerns for you to be aware of.

As a therapist I'm very aware that there are a number of minor ailments that can be directly linked to a person's balance of lifestyle. Many of these conditions can often be linked to poor nutrition even in the Western World where we have an abundance of food variety available. Through *awareness* these conditions can be treated naturally, simply by adjusting to a healthier balance of nutrition. When we are coping with stress or when we are unwell is a perfect time to make sure that we are getting the right amount of nutrients (including healthy portions of fresh air and sunshine!).

There's no doubt that the type of food we eat has an immediate impact on our health and well-being and is one of our main sources of energy for life, our FUEL. Therefore, the impact of what types of food we eat is just as important as the air we breathe.

Factually, too much protein in your diet can inhibit and tire the body. Interestingly, too little protein also causes fatigue and weakens the body as a whole. Too much or too little sugar also causes the same effects.

Our bodies (when we really begin to listen to them) can tell us what they need. Cravings aren't just experienced by pregnant ladies! When we're stressed or unwell it's surprising how we can learn about what our body *needs.*

Here are a few suggested tips:

- Try to buy organic fruit and vegetables whenever practical and affordable. Organic produce is grown in controlled conditions so it doesn't contain harmful pesticides and usually has more flavour.

- A good rule in recovery is to eat small, light meals at regular intervals. (Heavy meals take more time and energy to digest).

Try to have the following foods in **moderation**:

- Refined foods, which contain processed sugar such as biscuits, cakes, sugar in tea etc. After the initial surge of energy that sugar provides, blood sugar levels can plummet even further an hour or so after consumption. Therefore foods that contain processed sugars are best avoided as much as possible, or certainly taken in moderation to maintain a healthy balance and to reduce strain on our bodies.

- Processed or tinned foods, although there are some excellent exceptions of 'ready meals' now available. Watch the labels to be *aware* of additives. However, it is possible now to buy healthy prepared ready meals with no artificial ingredients thank goodness!

Many take-away foods contain additives and not many nutrients or vitamins. However, we didn't exclude them and used to treat ourselves now and again, to good old fish and chips. Thankfully, many takeaway food outlets now have much more awareness with regard to healthier eating so that's more good news.

The reason I'm a great believer in organic foods is that our soils in the UK and in many other countries have been farmed for so many years and with the use of pesticides, our soil has been depleted of much of its nutrients. Organic farming, thankfully, is becoming more popular and hopefully prices will decrease as its popularity grows. We now have more access to organic food sources and produce from all over the world more than ever before. Major supermarket chains are competing to produce the widest range of organic food and it's now pretty much possible to buy everything in organic form from tea, sugar, fruits and vegetables to meat, fish, eggs, dairy products, biscuits, cakes, chocolate to even wine.

An essential balance of carbohydrates, proteins, vitamins and minerals are highly important to our being and even more so when we're coping with stress and recovering from an illness. If we're feeling unwell or tired we may not feel up to preparing complicated meals, but the good news is that the foods we need the most at those times can be very simple to prepare.

Here are a few more tips:

- Eat as many different types of vegetables as possible in one sitting. (Exclude potatoes from the list of vegetables that you can eat freely, but include them as a main source of carbohydrate for energy.)

- Eating fresh fruit gives a slow release of natural sugars into our bloodstream and provides us with an excellent balance of energy throughout the day.

- Some fruits have lower amounts of sugars than others, such as peaches, pears, raspberries, strawberries and blueberries.

- Fruits with higher sugar content such as bananas, grapes and blackberries contain more sugar than many others so you don't need to eat so much of them to give yourself energy.

- Ideally steam vegetables if you can. Otherwise cook in a pan of unsalted boiling water to preserve their vitamin content.

- It's important to simply eat at the right times and never to skip meals to prevent fatigue. If you skip breakfast your blood sugar level can drop and you can become hypoglycaemic by about 11am. This can result in poor energy and concentration and tempt you to reach for a quick energy fix. In turn, it puts extra strain on the body as a whole. Fresh fruits are ideal breakfast foods providing slow release natural sugars and are also a great source of carbohydrate, a natural energy fuel for the body.

- Having a light nutritious lunch will prevent you from feeling extra sleepy in the afternoon.

Fresh fruit juice is an ideal way to start the day to provide a good intake of vitamins and is particularly good for children if they don't like cereals etc. Fresh fruits contain carbohydrate and sugars for energy. Ideally squeeze your own fruits. However, there are some fantastic and delicious juices available in supermarkets now. I recommend buying only the best, prepared from 100% pure juice and *not concentrate.*

With fresh juice the *life force* is retained and may the force be with you!

In yogic terms some foods are classed as '**tarismatic**' (*energy depleting*) and should be avoided or consumed in moderation. These are pickles, meats, spices, cheese, mushrooms and foods containing yeast.

Whereas foods which contain '**prana**' (*life energies*) are greatly encouraged. These are fresh fruit and vegetables (if limp, throw away because they will have lost most of their vitamin content and then they become tarismatic).

Vegetables, like us, contain living cells and the fresher they are the better they are for you.

Try to include lots of the following:

- Salads. Include as side salad dishes with fish and pasta as often as possible. Combining hot meats with salads makes a change and can be fun to experiment with.

- Pasta with homemade tomato sauce sprinkled with cheese or omelettes with fillings such as mushrooms, cheese, bacon or ham and cooked vegetables with cheese make a great alternative to meat. You could try out some vegetarian dishes and explore dishes from other countries. It's good to try new ideas and recipes for variety and balance. Variety in food also helps to stimulate your senses, smell, taste, sight and pure pleasure!

- Fresh casseroles and homemade soups, if possible. If not, those that contain no additives in cartons (not tins) are always good to include because of their nutritional value and ease of preparation.

- White meat, such as fresh chicken and turkey (not frozen), whenever possible.

- Fresh fish from the fishmongers. If you don't like fish it's the only time I would recommend you take a fish oil supplement, unless, of course you are allergic to fish. If that is the case try to make sure you include eggs and milk in your diet, which contain essential omega 3 oils.

- Whole foods, such as wholemeal bread, rye bread if you can't have wheat, whole-wheat pasta and wholegrain cereals, particularly those containing pro-biotic bacteria. Oat cereals, brown natural rice, jacket potatoes with tasty fillings. (Risottos are delicious and a great nutritious energy food and you can add lots of vegetables to them).

- Natural butter when possible, but obviously in moderation. Otherwise olive oil spread so long as it doesn't contain too many additives (check the labels).

- Eggs (maximum 2 in a week). I recommend buying free range and organic if possible. Use eggs boiled, poached or scrambled or in omelettes, which make fantastically nourishing light meals that are just the right amount of protein, are full of essential B vitamins and much more. Remember that the eggs from hens that roam in sunlight (just like us!) contain more vitamin D.

- Try to limit eating red meat to twice a week. Red meat takes much longer to digest, has been linked to certain cancers and can make you feel a bit fatigued. On a positive note red meat is a fantastic source of protein and energy and contains iron. The all important mineral for healthy blood, which in turn, helps to promote and maintain energy levels.

- The following in moderation: fresh lamb, pork, extra lean beef (no more than 1/2lb in a week), bacon (very little), ham and cheeses, (just a tiny cube about an inch square daily is enough for your daily calcium intake).

- Baked beans, I thoroughly recommend as a fabulous protein food that contains iron and they're great for the digestion too.

Try not to 'exclude' any food types from your diet. This is a perfect time to nourish your body like it's never been nourished or nurtured before.

- It's highly important to maintain balanced sugar levels; our moods and functions are immediately affected by any imbalance. Try to keep a check that you have a regular food intake and don't go for more than two hours without having some form of food or liquid refreshment.

- Try not to skip meals. If you aren't hungry, just have something light like a salad, vegetables or soup and a piece of fruit to minimise sugar cravings later on.

- Make sure you include a little salt in your diet (but try not to have more than the recommended 6 grams of salt in total each day) to keep your blood pressure level balanced. When the heat is on in summer be particularly aware of making extra sure you have a reasonable salt intake as we lose our natural salts through our perspiration.

- Try to make a healthy habit of resting after eating, by making sure you sit down for at least 15 minutes after a meal to conserve your energy while your stomach is busy digesting. Letting nature take its course!

Here are some great snack foods, which are low in fat and good for you (!):

Smoothies, yoghurts, nuts, dried fruits such as apricots, raisins, sultanas and dates (buy organic if possible), rice cakes with a little butter topped with fresh ham, smoked salmon or cream cheese with prawns, fresh fruits (especially bananas to satisfy hunger), cooked new potatoes, raw carrot and cucumber sticks (great for dipping in hummus).

The Importance of Natural Vitamins and Minerals for Healing

The key way to provide our bodies with the essential nutrients in the correct amounts is to eat balanced and varied diets. A simple lack of certain vitamins, minerals or amino acids required by the body can have an adverse affect on our health and well-being.

Vitamin supplements can help if your diet is particularly lacking in them. However, there's much controversy about their actual effect, and it's very important to be aware that care is needed with regard to excessive use of vitamin and mineral supplements. It may not be possible to be poisoned by a natural supplement overdose, but there is evidence that it *is* possible to overdose on synthetic vitamins, which can be toxic in excess. Many minor ailments like headaches, water retention, constipation and insomnia can be simply due to insufficient or excessive amounts vitamins. Just imagine how much less our wait in the doctors' surgeries could be through awareness!

Synthetic vitamins can cause imbalance and illness if taken in excess or even slightly in excess in some individuals. Also many contain artificial preservatives and colours.

Although we were advised to increase our vitamin intake, particularly vitamin C in fairly high doses, we only took supplements for about a week of our recovery and strongly believe that vitamin and mineral supplements are no substitute for nature's own found in many foods we eat.

All vitamins and minerals are essential for balanced health.

With regard to coping with stress and illness it's particularly important to include vitamin C and B complex vitamins in your diet.

Vitamin C (also known as ascorbic acid) is an essential water-soluble vitamin and therefore is easily destroyed by the cooking process. It may be affected by taking certain medicines (aspirin and cortisone) and if you smoke (one cigarette destroys 25 milligrams of it). Our bodies can't store it, so it serves a daily purpose. It stays within us for about three hours and any excess is expelled! It's important that you include it in your diet everyday. One of the signs of deficiency of vitamin C is fatigue.

Including vitamin C in your diet also helps decrease bad cholesterol and it's well known that it helps to build resistance against bacterial and viral infections. It also helps wounds to heal, accelerating the healing process, particularly after surgery and helps to reduce the incidence of blood clots in veins.

The great news is that vitamin C is available in fresh fruit and vegetables in abundance and the following are particularly good sources:

- Kiwi fruits and citrus fruits (oranges, lemons and grapefruit, I suggest you try pink grapefruit for its sweetness) and all types of berries. All fresh fruits have many more vitamins and minerals included. A lack of fruit in the diet alone can cause symptoms of fatigue. Fresh fruit is a rich source of natural sugar and carbohydrate so makes an ideal breakfast food alone.

- Many vegetables, but most notably cauliflower, broccoli, potatoes, green peppers, tomatoes, Brussels sprouts and parsley.

Just by drinking a glass of 100% natural orange juice in the morning gives you half a days supply.

What's interesting to know also is that taking a vitamin C *supplement* at night may disturb your sleep. However, it can be recommended in large quantity supplements for the treatment of various disorders with some great results.

B Complex Vitamins

The function of B vitamins is to maintain a healthy nervous system and to help utilize carbohydrates. These may be found in the following:

Brewer's yeast, bacon, oatmeal, spinach, broccoli, peanuts, eggs, honey, milk, oysters, eggs, rice, wheat, bran, liver, tomatoes, almonds, wheat germ, kidney, beef, poultry, cheese, potatoes, pork, most vegetables, milk, cabbage, fish, and cantaloupe melon.

Minerals

As well as a balanced diet the important minerals that are 'extra' beneficial to include when coping and recovering from M.E./C.F.S., stress, anxiety and depression are:

Calcium

As well as being highly important for maintaining healthy bones and teeth, calcium is also exceptionally good for the health of all the nerves, muscles and blood and may be found in:

Cheese, milk, yoghurt, eggs, root vegetables, fruits, wholemeal flour, fish and pulses (beans).

Iodine

Which is often found lacking in people who are suffering from fatigue is excellent for healthy thyroid function and metabolic rate, iodine helps to strengthen hair, teeth, nails and the skin and is found in:

Seafood, dried fruits and leafy green vegetables, especially spinach.

Iron

This is essential for the formation of haemoglobin in your blood which transports oxygen and helps to keep your energy levels balanced. Iron is found in:

Dark leafy vegetables such as watercress, spinach and greens; dried fruits especially raisins, dates, beans, pulses, red meat and offal.

Magnesium

Which is also often lacking in people suffering from fatigue can be found (you may be delighted to hear!) in:

Chocolate and cocoa, whole grains (rice and bread) and dried fruits (organic preferably), particularly apricots and prunes.

Phosphorus

Often lacking in people if suffering from stress can be found in:

Cheese, egg yolk, sardines, tuna, seafood and meat.

Potassium

This is essential for the balance of water within our cells and an activator for energy production and nerve impulses. Can be found in:

Bananas, dried fruits, cereals, fruit juices, nuts, raw salad, cheese, brown rice, wholemeal flour and traces are found in tea, coffee and chocolate.

Selenium

Excellent for detoxification, selenium helps to remove heavy metals and is believed to help slow down the aging process. It is found in:

Wheat germ, whole grain rice and wheat, yeast, pineapples, meat, fish, shellfish and ginseng.

Power Foods

In addition to the suggested fresh fruits, vegetables, proteins and carbohydrates you should include in your daily diet, there are fruits, vegetables and herbs that possess special healing properties and are ideal to include in the diet, if you are coping and recovering from anything! I've listed them here for easy reference.

Apples

Apples are an excellent source of vitamins and provide the perfect carbohydrates so are ideal for breakfast. They contain vitamins B2, B3 and E, calcium, phosphorus, potassium, zinc, folic acid and magnesium and also help to cleanse and remove toxins.

Apricots

Contain magnesium, copper, calcium, potassium, folic acid, vitamin C, beta-carotene, and iron. Organic apricots can now be found in supermarkets with no additives.

Asparagus

Recommended highly for recovery and maintenance, asparagus is rich in vitamin C, potassium and beta-carotene (which can help to prevent cancer).

Avocado

I couldn't recommend this more highly for recovery! These little gems are wonderful for any nerve-related disorders, stress, fatigue or 'burn out' of any kind. They are naturally high in mono-unsaturated fatty acids for sustaining your energy levels.

Bananas

A high-energy fruit, crammed with vitamins and minerals, bananas are also an excellent source of potassium. An excellent all-round fruit to help balance your energy levels.

Beetroot

Strangely, I had a recurring craving for beetroot, even late at night. It proved, once again, to be just what the doctor ordered. Try in the raw or cooked (no vinegar) in slices with dollops of mayonnaise and a tiny sprinkling of salt. My darling Mum prepares sliced beets in vinegar layered with finely sliced raw onions. Marinate for at least two hours so that juices and flavours can penetrate one another then use as a side salad dish. Words fail me as to how delicious and healthy this recipe is! Beetroot contains magnesium, calcium, iron, potassium, manganese, folic acid and vitamin C and is said to lower harmful cholesterol levels. It's nearly overqualified for the power foods list!

Beans and Pulses

Baked beans, as I've already mentioned, are an excellent source of protein. Included in this category are also kidney beans, broad beans and green beans, in fact as many varieties of beans as possible.

Blueberries

Blueberries have a great vitamin C and beta-carotene content and are reputed to have an antioxidant effect. Blueberries benefit your eyesight and also help with blood cleansing and improving the circulation. Altogether they're absolutely perfect for beating M.E./ C.F.S., depression, anxiety and stress- related illness.

Carrots

Carrots contain a rich source of beta-carotene (pro-vitamin A), calcium, potassium and phosphorus. They are excellent for the health of the liver and digestive tract. They help kidney function and destroy bacteria and viruses so are superb detoxifiers. They also help to improve vision and skin elasticity. Try to buy organic whenever possible, the difference in flavour is amazing!

Cauliflower, Broccoli, Brussels sprouts and Cabbage

Otherwise known as the brassica group of vegetables. These are a strong cancer preventing group of vegetables which contain powerful antioxidants and high levels of vitamin C.

Chillies

Chillies contain powerful antioxidants and, apparently, to combat the burning sensation that chilli peppers cause when eaten, the brain secretes endorphins, a natural euphoric drug that produces a sensation of well-being. It's the same hormone that is secreted after an orgasm so brace yourself!

Chocolate

The wonderful effect of cocoa on the central nervous system has been known for years. With it's powerful properties it helps us to release the 'feel good' hormone serotonin into our blood streams relaxing us blissfully. It can be relaxing as well as stimulating and provides a fantastic 'pick-me-up' at any time of day. Chocolate contains a substance called (theobromaine) similar to caffeine so is mildly addictive! It also has a high magnesium content and its sugar content also makes chocolate a great sedative. There's also research that the monounsaturated fatty acids in chocolate help to reduce the amount of harmful cholesterol in our blood and increase the levels of beneficial cholesterol. It also contains properties which help to protect vascular walls.

Many of the delicious organic chocolate bars available today are very high in cocoa solids and it's possible to experience the benefits of eating this amazing substance in just a few small pieces. Which prompts another saying, "It's the quality not the quantity which counts". No wonder we get chocolate cravings, it gets all our hormones out to play!

Eggs

Eggs include protein, amino acids, nicotinic acid, calcium, iron, phosphorus, sodium and vitamins A, B 1 (thiamine) B 2 (riboflavin) and vitamin D.

Fish

Fish is a first class source of protein, calcium, phosphorous, nicotinic acid, vitamins A and D and has traces of fluorine and iodine. Oily fish such as herring, salmon, mackerel and sardines contain rich amounts of fatty acids called omega-3 and are extremely beneficial to balance the immune system, reduce harmful cholesterol, protect veins and arteries, can even reduce the risk of heart attack and help to alleviate migraine pain.

Elizabeth Bailey

Tinned tuna, sardines and pilchards are good but they contain less omega 3 fish oil because the fish has the fat removed before canning. Recent studies recommended that you should take a supplement if your diet is lacking in any of the following foods in which Omega 3 oils may be found: fish, milk and eggs. There's also the theory that eating fish can increase fertility chances but this hasn't yet been recorded as a scientific fact (as far as I know!) however, south sea fisherman swear it does just that!

During and after the last world war *fish liver oil* supplements were taken but people were experiencing rationing then. We surely can't use that as an excuse now. We have the most wonderful and varied range of foods available than at any other time. Besides, I'm sure many would agree that the taste of freshly cooked fish beats fish liver oil taken on a spoon any day!

Honey

This is a wonderful natural source of sugar with healing and anti-bacterial properties, which go back centuries. The Romans used to put honey on open wounds to heal them and keep them free from infection. Look for pure honey and I recommend taking a teaspoonful at least three times a week for the rest of your life.

Kiwi Fruit

Absolutely packed with vitamin C, kiwi fruit has the highest amount of vitamin C than any fruit, even after a week or so sitting in the fruit basket.

Lemons and Limes

A great way to include these vitamin C packed little treasures and to enjoy them at their best is to add fresh slices to cool filtered water or mineral water and sip throughout the day. They're also delicious squeezed freshly over salads and are excellent fat busters too. Of course, if you allow yourself the odd indulgence, you can't beat a gin and tonic with ice and a slice of either ~ besides, it beats sucking them!

Mangos and Exotic Fruits

These are all fantastic for supplying vitamins and essential slow-release natural sugars. They contain beta-carotene and are a good source of vitamin C and have blood-cleansing properties.

Melons

Melons contain calcium, potassium, phosphorus, vitamin C, beta-carotene and magnesium and are excellent for re-hydrating.

Milk

Use whole milk if possible, and in moderation. Whole milk has higher calcium levels than skimmed milk. Skimmed milk, however, is said to help prevent the liver from producing excess cholesterol and helps to lower blood pressure. Milk contains vitamins A, B-Complex, D and E, as well as the hormone melatonin and lactose, a natural sugar compound. It is an excellent protein food and interestingly organic milk contains more omega 3 than regular milk.

Milk Products, Cheese, Yoghurt and Butter

When consumed in moderation, these provide a vital supply of calcium, vitamins and protein. Calcium enriched soya milk is a great alternative if you can't have milk from animals.

Mushrooms

Mushrooms contain calcium, iron, vitamins B3 and B5, folic acid, magnesium and zinc. Good for thinning the blood and can help to lower cholesterol and helps the immune and nervous system.

Nuts

If you're lucky enough to be able to eat them, I wholeheartedly suggest you include them at this crucial time. They have many great properties, but like everything, eat in moderation, as they contain a lot of fat. Nuts contain protein, vitamins, minerals and oils.

They can also cause lethargy if you eat too many (those squirrels certainly know how to live!).

Oats

Highly nutritious and recommended for people who are convalescing, growing children and athletes, oats are fantastic for bones and connective tissue maintenance. Reported to help balance cholesterol levels (they lower bad cholesterol and raise *beneficial* cholesterol). Oats contain calcium, phosphorous, iron, manganese, vitamin B5 and folic acid. They also have high fibre content. They help to regulate high blood *pressure* and to lower high blood *sugar* levels and are known as one of nature's best anti- depressants.

Olives

Green and black, olives contain iron, beta-carotene and calcium. They're good for the liver and gall bladder and help the body to increase the secretion of bile to aid digestion.

Onions

Onions contain folic acid, calcium, magnesium, phosphorous, potassium and beta-carotene. They are highly recommended for detoxifying as they can help to remove parasites and heavy metals. They also have antiseptic and antibiotic properties and can help to reduce asthma. Onions are also great if you have a cold, they make your nose and eyes run even more which helps to flush out viruses.

Oranges

Oranges contain calcium, beta-carotene, folic acid, potassium and vitamin C. They are good source of vitamin C for immune defence and help to stimulate peristalsis (digestive muscle contractions) so are good for detoxifying.

Papayas

A good source of calcium, potassium, vitamin C, beta-carotene and magnesium. Papayas are excellent for aiding the digestion and helping to soothe intestinal inflammation. They are also good for detoxifying and have cancer-preventing properties.

Peas

Peas are high in protein and essential vitamins, especially vitamin C.

Peppers

Like them or not they contain exquisitely high levels of vitamins A, B and C (red peppers contain more vitamin C and beta-carotene than green peppers) and are great for healthy nails, skin and hair. Look up chillies for the other great reasons to include them in your diet!

Peaches and Nectarines

Both are easy to digest and are rich in vitamin A and carotene. They are delicious and beautifully fragrant fruits which all helps to stimulate our senses.

Potatoes

They are full of vitamin C and are an amazing carbohydrate fuel, exactly right for what you need. It's best to bake them and eat their skins where most of the nutrients are to be found. I suggest you try sweet potatoes too. They're so good baked that they don't need much added to them other than a little butter.

Prunes

Prunes contain powerful antioxidants that help to counteract damage from free radicals and are a fantastic source of fibre. Like many other dried fruits, try to buy organically produced prunes to avoid preservatives.

Raisins

Raisins provide an excellent supply of iron and fibre (you only need a few to benefit) and they're an ideal snack food.

Raspberries

A particularly good choice of fruit because they're packed with vitamins B and C, also manganese, magnesium, folic acid, potassium and copper. They are also lower in sugar than many other fruits making them ideal for maintaining balanced blood sugar levels.

Salads

Try to have a side salad with meals as much as possible, not just in summer when they can turn into main courses. Salad goes well with pasta, fish, bolognaise, chilli, jacket potatoes and rice dishes. Try adding freshly squeezed lemon juice as a dressing for an extra zing. **Lettuce** contains anti-carcinogenic substances and has been known for many years to be a mild sedative; it's perfect at the end of a stressy day! Apparently it's better to eat salad at the beginning of a meal as it increases bile secretions, but that's getting a bit too technical. I suggest you just eat as much salad as you can, whenever you can.

Sesame Seeds

An interesting little addition for salads, sesame seeds contain nutrients that are beneficial for brain and nerve cells. They are a good source of natural oils which help to maintain a healthy nervous system.

Sunflower Seeds

Sunflower seeds are excellent if you are suffering from general weakness and are helpful for growing children. They also contain essential natural oils.

Spinach

Spinach is immensely good for you. Try to get into the habit of having raw spinach (many prepared bags of salad leaves now contain spinach). Add a few raw leaves to meals now and again. Spinach is a great source of iron and vitamin C.

Tea and Coffee

Tea is a powerful antioxidant. It's been recommended if recovering from M.E./C.F.S. to have decaffeinated tea and coffee, but to be honest I found it better to have good old fashioned what I call - builders tea! I found that it helped to pick me up. What I do strongly recommend is not to drink tea or coffee after about 4pm as it does perk you up and you need all the decent sleep you can get. It's a case of experiment with anything that I suggest to your own liking, but all within *moderation.* Interestingly, coffee as well as tea actually has traces of vitamins, riboflavin and nicotinic acid and minerals potassium, calcium, magnesium, iron, copper and sulphur.

Instant coffee is richer in minerals than ground coffee as it's concentrated. Coffee is also reputed to help stave off heart problems and can help ease fatigue. As with tea, coffee is a stimulant and both taken in large quantities can be addictive. I would recommend a maximum of three cups of either daily.

Tomatoes

Tomatoes are rich in vitamins and minerals, mainly pro-vitamin A and vitamin C. They contain natural fibre and are fantastic for strengthening the body and are often used in the treatment for anaemia. Tomatoes can help the body to fight infection as they have a diuretic effect, dissolving uric acid and helping to eliminate urea. They can also help to relieve constipation and can help if you suffer from water retention.

Watercress

Another fantastic vegetable and again highly recommended for combating fatigue and stress related illness, watercress is very rich in iron for healthy blood and for the nervous system. It also contains iodine, phosphorus and vitamins A and C.

Whole Grains

Bread, flour, pasta, wholegrain natural rice all contain valuable B vitamins, nutrients and immensely important fibre, to soak up any nastiness in the digestive system. Rye is also good (rye crackers can be used instead of bread).

Limiting your bread intake to maximum 2 slices every other day can help to prevent too much bloating which can zap your energy. I also recommend never adding bran to your cereal as it has the same effect as swallowing bits of a scouring pad to your system!

Wine (red in particular)

Just have to mention it! There's lots of evidence that a glass of red wine actually reduces bad cholesterol, and, in fact, I read recently that there's a heart surgeon in the U.K. who insists that patients should have a glass of it each day after surgery. It has a great fat-busting effect when accompanying fatty foods, not to mention its great relaxing effect, in moderation of course.

Wine can be added to gravies, casseroles, bolognaise and chilli. Along with tomatoes, wine cuts through grease brilliantly and is also said to help lower harmful cholesterol levels – bottoms up!

The Magical Healing Properties of Everyday Herbs

There are some fantastic therapeutic herbs that can help the healing process and can be used regularly in cooking. Even the smell of a cupboard containing herbs is something I'm sure one could become addicted to! Pleasant natural smells excite the pleasure areas of our brain so it's all positive news!

I've included the herbs that are easy to obtain and can be used in many dishes and most importantly those that have healing effects which are ideal for coping and recovery from M.E./C.F.S., anxiety, depression and stress related conditions.

Basil

A wonderfully balancing herb as it's said to first stimulate the brain, sharpen the memory and nervous system and then calms them down! In some Mediterranean countries it's believed that if eaten with an evening meal, it helps to promote a good night's sleep and that drinking it as a tea in the morning can encourage alertness. It goes really well mixed with tomatoes or snipped over salads, pasta or in soups and is delightful with carrots, courgettes, onions or potatoes and a little butter.

Cinnamon

Cinnamon is useful to restore energy and excellent for helping get rid of colds. It can be sprinkled into red meat dishes (shepherds pie, bolognaise etc.) and it's surprising where you can sneak it in. It's equally good on creamy rice pudding or on buttered toast.

Coriander

A useful and neutral warming tonic at anytime, coriander is easily found in prepared salads from supermarkets.

Garlic

Thousands of years ago cloves of garlic were given to workers building the pyramids in Egypt to keep their energy high and to ward off illnesses such as colds and flu. Garlic helps the body to eliminate harmful bacteria, is a great natural expectorant and also causes a vasodilatation effect helping to increase the circulation, warming cold limbs, lowering high blood pressure and helping to unclog blocked arteries. It just hits the spot for recovering from M.E./C.F.S., anxiety, depression and stress related conditions.

Ginger

Ginger aids digestion, warms the body and helps to clear the lungs. It's great for combating nausea (if you have children who suffer car sickness give them a ginger biscuit half an hour before your journey, it works miraculously). It also helps the circulation and is reputed to clear blocked energies in the body.

Horseradish

Again, a stimulant with a warming effect, horseradish is a *must* with beef, cooked in any way. Effective action for colds or anyone with weak energy or poor circulation – in other words - just right!

Marjoram

Naturally warming, toning and relaxing, marjoram relieves tiredness and tension. It helps with a lack of energy and is good snipped over cooked vegetables, especially carrots.

Mint

A cooling, refreshing, fantastic herb. Its scent alone has an awakening and stimulating effect. Mint helps with digestive problems and stimulates the appetite. You can buy peppermints containing real peppermint oil and add chopped mint to many vegetables, like dreamily minted peas and new potatoes. It has a great balancing effect on the body, increasing vitality and inducing relaxation.

Parsley

A fresh tasting, mild stimulant and tonic herb, with high vitamin content rich in pro-vitamin A (contains even more than carrots). It's also high in vitamin C and iron. Parsley helps to purify the blood and is a mild diuretic, so it's good for helping to combat water retention. It dilates blood vessels and helps to strengthen muscle tissue in the intestines, urinary tract and the uterus. It also helps to eliminate intestinal parasites, combats anaemia and stimulates the appetite. Chop and sprinkle on to salads and cooked vegetable dishes. Parsley is good for seasoning meat and fish and is simply *made* for a big pile of fresh prawns on a slice of French bread!

Rosemary

Reputed to move energy around the body and improve circulation, rosemary has been used for many years as a tonic and can be used in many dishes. It's excellent cooked with roast lamb and is said to sharpen the memory. Nervous weakness and depression are also helped by rosemary – what a girl! Perfect for M.E./ C.F.S. and stress related conditions.

Sage

Sage is supposed to be one of the best remedies for fighting poor concentration and depression and helps to speed up recovery from any debilitating disease and in convalescence. It's also said to help to strengthen the lungs and is especially good if you are suffering from colds, coughs and flu, particularly if your symptoms include a sore throat. A perfect herb with five star healing properties.

Tarragon

Tarragon is a wonderful balancing herb. It mildly stimulates the nervous system and at the same time calms it. Also good for tummy upsets caused by stress and nervous tension. Snip over salads or cooked vegetables, or use in casseroles. It's great with chicken and fish, added to omelettes and creamy soups ~ *dreamy.*

Breakfast Suggestions

Because eating breakfast is *so* important in helping to maintain balance of our metabolism, I'd like to give out some suggestions for what you could eat. If you don't have much of an appetite for breakfast 'smoothies' are a great way to start the day and are full of vitamins, minerals and essential carbohydrates. By giving yourself a variety of foods you'll be getting an even better balance of nutrients.

E.g. Day 1 could be:

Melon with a slice or two of orange on the top

A slice of wholemeal toast with Marmite or whatever you like on toast!

English breakfast tea (organic preferably)

Day 2

Porridge made with whole milk and a teaspoonful of acacia honey

A glass of fresh fruit juice

Day 3

Fresh fruit salad made with at least three different fruits and drenched in the freshly squeezed juice from 1 orange

2 rye biscuit slices (like Ryvita) spread lightly with olive oil spread topped with a slice of ham from the deli counter (avoid pre packed foods whenever possible) and slices of fresh tomato

Organic ground coffee made with half hot water and half warm milk

Day 4

Cereal containing pro-biotic bacteria to help the friendly bacteria in your stomach

A piece of fresh fruit

English breakfast tea

Day 5

Plain natural Greek yoghurt with a swirl of acacia honey and a few fresh raspberries

One or two rice cakes with a little butter and smooth peanut butter or Marmite

Fruit Tea

Day 6

A cooked breakfast of grilled lean bacon, poached egg, grilled tomatoes, button mushrooms cooked in a tiny amount of butter (can't beat it for taste!) and a slice of wholemeal toast with marmalade or apricot conserve

Fresh fruit juice

Day 7

Ham and Emmental cheese bagel

Organic ground coffee made with warm milk

Or melon balls or slices garnished with grapes and jumbo orange slices

Toast and organic honey or preserves

Why not try a *different* fruit juice or a smoothie?

Ideas for hot extras to tickle your taste buds:

Smoked Haddock with poached egg

(Choose fresh smoked and not artificially smoked fish from the fish counter)

Wholemeal toast and butter

Mushrooms with a difference!

(Mushrooms poached in milk on wholemeal toast with tomato ketchup relish).

Simply melt some butter in a non-stick saucepan and sauté mushrooms for about a minute then

add a little milk to poach them for 1 minute.
Mix so that the milk turns a mushroom colour.
Serve onto hot buttered wholemeal toast with a
little grated cheese if you fancy.

Poached egg on wholemeal toast

With grilled crispy bacon rashers with brown
sauce

Giant grilled mushrooms

Stuffed with cream cheese, breadcrumbs and
garden chives

And there are eggs of course. Boiled, poached
or scrambled egg with wholemeal soldiers and
sweet or savoury omelettes.

Recipes

Try to include plenty of carbohydrates in your diet and minimise eating meat to once a day.

I've included a few of my favourite recipes here because they're delicious, nutritious and simple to prepare.

Favourite suggested salads:

- Baked salmon, new potatoes and peas with a herb salad.
- Hot chicken or other fresh sliced hot meat, salad and herbs with Lyonnaise potatoes.
- Fresh ham or cold meat salad (from the deli counter, not pre-packed) with a jacket potato with butter or olive oil spread or a sprinkle of grated cheese.
- Grilled mackerel with salad and wholemeal bread and butter.

There's one thing I simply 'must' tell you about!

Fresh Vegetable Water

Whenever you cook vegetables, I suggest cook as many together in one saucepan at a time to make a nutritious vegetable water drink. You could either use it for this vitamin packed drink or use it as stock for soups or casseroles. Never add extra salt when cooking vegetables it destroys some of the vitamins and definitely not recommended for vegetable water drink.

Boil some freshly drawn filtered water, a small amount depending on the amount of vegetables. Add all your vegetables, the more the merrier! When your vegetables are cooked, drain the vegetable water into a mug and add a few teaspoonfuls of Bovril (according to taste) or a similar vegetarian version and mix. Drink immediately, as often as you can!

(Drinking is one of the fastest ways we are able to absorb food, so it's a fantastic way to get vitamins and minerals into your body at record speed!)

Elizabeth Bailey

Fresh Homemade Soup

(Great as a pick-me-up, my family beg me to make this in the winter!)

Serves 2-4 depending upon the quantity of vegetables you use

Ingredients:
Extra virgin olive oil
2 large onions
A selection of peeled and chopped root vegetables e.g. carrots, swede, parsnip and potatoes
A selection of green vegetables e.g. Savoy cabbage, Brussels sprouts, broccoli and celery
1½ pints (900ml) of hot vegetable bouillon (alternatively you could use beef or chicken bouillon)
Worcestershire sauce
1 tablespoon of tomato puree
Seasoning
A pinch of chilli powder to taste (optional)
A sprig of watercress to garnish

Method:

Finely chop two large onions and fry in a large saucepan in the olive oil. When the onion is soft add the root vegetables. Gently sauté for a few minutes. Add the stock and simmer for 15 minutes.

Add the green vegetables and a dash or two of Worcestershire sauce, the tomato puree and chilli powder. Stir well. Bring to the boil then simmer for just 5 minutes to preserve all those lovely vitamins in the vegetables. Liquidate the mixture in a food mixer or in a blender. You can make it as thick as you like by using more vegetables or blending it for a shorter period of time. Finally season to taste.

This soup is great served with toasted crusty bread with melted cheese and a sprig of watercress. This soup will do you the power of good and it's good fun to experiment and try different varieties of vegetables each time to suit your individual taste.

Most of all enjoy!

Elizabeth Bailey

Lamb Hot Pot

(Mouth-wateringly lovely, just add your favourite root vegetables)

Serves 2

Ingredients:
2 lamb loin chops
1 large onion
1 large carrot
4 medium sized potatoes
1 tablespoon of extra virgin olive oil
A sprig of fresh thyme or rosemary
Seasoning to taste
A sprinkling of seasoned wholemeal or plain flour on a plate
1 vegetable bouillon cube mixed with ¾ pint (450ml) boiling water
1 glass red wine and preferably one to sip whilst cooking!
1oz (25g) butter
1 tablespoon of tomato puree
Worcestershire sauce

Pre-heat oven to about 180c/350f /gas 4

Method:
Peel and slice the onion and carrot into rings and gently fry both in the oil for about 2-3 minutes until onion is soft, then put aside.

Dip the lamb loin chops in a little seasoned (preferably whole wheat) flour and fry for about 1-2 minutes on each side until slightly golden to seal in the flavour and juices.

Peel and slice 4 medium sized potatoes into thin rings.

Put half of the carrot and onion mixture on the base of a greased casserole dish, followed by a layer of sliced potatoes (about half). Place the lamb on top. Add the sprig of fresh thyme or rosemary and season with salt and pepper. Finish with a further layer of the carrot and onion mixture and finish with a layer of potatoes.

Add two or three dashes of Worcester sauce and the wine to the stock to make up 1pint of liquid. Add the tomato puree and pour over the other ingredients in the casserole dish. Dot with butter and cover with a lid or foil and bake in oven for about 1 1/2 hours. Remove the lid or foil and continue to cook for about 30 minutes until the potatoes start to brown.

Remove the herb sprigs and serve with cooked or pickled red cabbage, petit pois and sugar snap peas.

Provencal Style Chicken Casserole

Make this dish with as many root vegetables as possible and mushrooms. (Mushrooms are a wonderful addition to casseroles to give richness). The quantities I suggested are approximate. Have fun and experiment as much as possible. Add more or less of what you like depending on how many you are cooking for and the size of your casserole dish!

Serves 2

Ingredients:
2 fresh chicken breasts
6 oz (175g) baby carrots or 1-2 medium carrots peeled sliced
Baby new potatoes
4-5oz (125 /150g) lean rindless bacon
9 oz (275g) button mushrooms
2 tablespoons of plain wholemeal or white flour
1oz (25g) butter
1 tablespoon of extra virgin olive oil
¾ pint (450ml) chicken stock made from bouillon cube
¼ pint (150 ml) dry white wine
A sprinkling of dried tarragon or 1 fresh bay leaf or two dried bay leaves (discard before serving)
¼ pint (150 ml) single cream (use less if you don't want it to be too rich)

Pre-heat oven to about 180c/350f /gas 4

Method:

Rinse the chicken under running water and pat dry with kitchen paper. Place the flour and seasoning onto a plate and lightly coat the chicken pieces, shaking off any excess.

Heat the butter and oil in a non-stick frying pan and lightly fry the chicken pieces (only for a minute or two) until golden. Remove and set aside.

Peel and cut the onion in half then into three so you have six nice sized chunks. Rinse and dry the carrots and potatoes, if you're not using baby carrots, peel and slice the others. Wash the mushrooms in a sieve and cut the bacon into wide strips.

Fry the onion, carrots, bacon and mushrooms in the remaining oil of the pan and cook for 3-4 minutes until the onions are soft. Then add the wine and stock and bring to the boil, stirring all the time.

Return the chicken to a casserole dish and add all the vegetable ingredients and a sprig of tarragon or the bay leaves. Turn the oven down to about (150c, 300f, gas 2) and cook for about 2 hours, checking half way through and stirring as necessary.

Just before serving remove the tarragon sprigs or bay leaves, stir in the cream and season well.

Serve with thinly sliced green beans, finely shredded Savoy cabbage, and chunks of crusty French bread.

* * *

Braised Beef with Onions and Mushrooms

This cooks for hours, so you can chill out. It's a totally melt-in-the-mouth meal. This recipe couldn't be simpler and the longer it cooks on a low heat the more melt-in-the-mouth it becomes!

Serves 2-3

Ingredients:
1lb (450g) lean braising beef cubed
1 large onion
6-8oz (170-250g) button mushrooms
1-pint (500ml) beef bouillon stock
Seasoning
Worcester sauce
1 glass of red wine (optional)
1 tablespoon extra virgin olive oil
1 tablespoon of flour
Water
A sprinkle of nutmeg

Pre-heat Oven to about 200c/350f/gas 4

Method:
Heat the oil in a non-stick frying pan and briefly fry the meat until it starts to brown, to seal in all the flavour. Place into a casserole dish and cover.

Fry remaining onions and mushrooms until the onions soften.

Add a few dashes of Worcester sauce and the nutmeg to the beef stock. Carefully combine the flour with a little water to make a paste and when it's combined add this mixture to the stock.

Put remaining vegetables into the casserole dish, drench with the stock mixture (if you're cheeky like me) add the glass of wine and cook on a high oven (200c, 400f, gas 6) for half an hour.

Turn right down to about (160c, 325f, gas 3) depending on how fierce your oven can get! Cook very slowly for 2 –3 hours, checking every hour or so.

Serve with mild vegetables like courgettes, carrots, and broad beans with boiled or new potatoes.

Prawn and Rice Salad

Serves 2-3

Ingredients:

1 pint (600ml) of cooked and peeled fresh prawns
1 mug of dried rice
1 red pepper de-seeded and chopped finely
½ cucumber chopped finely
2 spring onions chopped finely into tiny rings
Fresh parsley to decorate
A sprinkle of paprika (optional)

Method:

Simply boil the rice according to the instructions on the pack and leave to cool slightly. Then mix the rice with the other ingredients (it helps to combine the flavours if the rice is still slightly warm).

Top with the fresh parsley, fantastic any time of the year and great for parties.

Serve with warm crusty warm bread from the oven and butter.

Chicken and Mushroom Parcels

Serves 2

Ingredients:
2 skinless chicken breasts
1-2 large onions chopped finely
4-5oz (125-150g) chopped mushrooms
A little butter
Seasoning to taste

Aluminium cooking foil (always use the matt side next to the food)

Pre-heat oven to 180c/350f/gas 4

Method:
Wash the chicken and pat it dry with kitchen paper. Cut out individual squares of foil to wrap each piece of chicken. Place a layer of chopped mushrooms onto the foil followed by the onion. Place a chicken breast on top with a good teaspoonful of butter and season to taste.

Wrap the individual parcels loosely leaving room for the heat to circulate and a small hole in the top for the steam to escape.

Place the parcels on a baking tray and cook in pre-heated oven for approx 40-45 minutes until the chicken is cooked thoroughly. Then turn out onto warm plates and pour the delicious cooking juices all over.

Serve with tasty selection of vegetables and new potatoes.

Elizabeth Bailey

Salmon with Ginger

Serves 2

Ingredients:
2 fresh salmon fillets
Marinade:
Sprinkle of ground ginger or a little grated fresh ginger
to taste
Juice and zest of 1 lemon
Crushed garlic or finely chopped spring onions
Seasoning

Dill to decorate

Pre heat oven to 180c/350f/gas 4

Method:
Simply mix all marinade ingredients together and
cover salmon fillets with the mixture. Cover lightly
with foil and cook on a baking tray for approx 15-20
minutes until the salmon is cooked through. Serve with
seasonal vegetables and creamed potatoes.

Grilled Fresh Mackerel

(Heaps of Omega 3 oils – excellent health benefits and highly recommended!)

Serves 2

Ingredients:
2 Fresh mackerel fillets
Freshly grated breadcrumbs
1 egg
Slice of fresh lemon for garnish and flavour

Method:
Simply take the mackerel fillets, dip them into the beaten egg and cover in fresh breadcrumbs. Grill on a Pyrex (heat resistant) plate for 10 minutes or until cooked through. Serve with a dash of lemon juice and a side salad.

Baked Salmon, Mackerel or Trout

Serves 2

Ingredients:
2 fish fillets
Butter
Seasoning

Pre heat oven to 180c/350f/gas 4

Method:
Simply bake the filleted and cleaned fish fillets in foil parcels with a knob of butter and a little seasoning to taste, in a hot oven for about 20-25 minutes, making sure the fish is cooked through. Serve with new or creamed potatoes and fresh vegetables.

* * *

Water
Water contains 'Prana' - Life Force Energy

Just a couple of words about Adams Ale! Increasing your water intake can greatly improve your overall health and well-being. As well as de-toxifying our systems, clearing our internal tubes and refreshing every living cell, organism and tissue within our bodies with life sustaining energy and essential minerals.

Keeping hydrated by drinking more water can have a significant effect on our energy levels and clarity of thought.

Our bodies are made up of 70% water. Just by taking a look at plants we can *see* when they need to be watered, but dehydration in the human body isn't so obvious. Studies show that being just 2% dehydrated can affect our performance and concentration.

To capture maximum energy flow 'prana' (life force) from your supply, run the tap before taking water to drink or cook with. As the water flows freely through the main water systems it has more oxygen life force in it and you're directly taking the energy flow into your body. I suggest filtering all cold tap water for drinking/ cooking as this eliminates much of the chlorine and harmful metals and makes water taste beautifully clean. Keep the fresh water in the fridge and replace filters as necessary and check manufacturer's instructions.

It's recommended that we include drinking at least 6 to 8 glasses (or up to 2 litres of water a day) depending on our frame. This can be included in watered down juices, fruit or herbal teas and should be sipped throughout the day so as not to put too much strain on the kidneys. To start, I would suggest drinking just 2 extra glasses from day one and work to increase your intake gradually. In hot weather sip more water than usual throughout the day maybe with some ice and a slice of lime or lemon to add some extra flavour.

Try to keep hydrated and top up and conserve your energies by drinking a glass of water before, during and after exercise, even when you've been walking.

When you start to drink more water you may find that you need to use the toilet more often. This is a brilliant sign from your body that it's responding by detoxifying. Another good test is to look at the colour of your urine; basically the darker it is the more toxins need to be thrown out. When you are eating well and drinking sufficient water your urine should be pale yellow in colour…so that's another positive thing to aim for!

I must mention the fantastic liver cleansing benefits of grapefruit juice. Pink grapefruit is sweeter and I suggest you try 100% pure juice and not juice made from concentrate. It's a great way to cleanse your liver first thing in the morning. Try to include a couple of glasses a week in your diet. Pineapple juice is also beneficial especially if you suffer from asthma as it contains special properties which can help to dilate the bronchial tubes as well as being packed with vitamins and minerals.

- In the morning a great pick me up for your liver and to clear the system, is to add ice and a slice and a squeeze of fresh lemon or lime to a glass of fresh water ~ just keep the fruit in the fridge till next day. In no time at all your eyes and skin should be clearer and you'll look and feel even more gorgeous than ever.

Alcohol

Everything in moderation we're all aware. Alcohol can become self destructive if taken in excess and can lead to health problems. It depletes us of vital B vitamins and much needed vitamin C, which are so important to maintain healthy nervous and immune systems. In excess its effects can cause panic and anxiety attacks, headaches and depression, so not exactly what we need right now!

However, all is not lost. I am a great believer in a little of what you fancy does you good. We all have choices and on the road to my recovery I found that a gradual introduction of a glass of red wine with a meal, or a sweet sherry now and again, was a great pick-me-up and helped to both relax and cheer me up. My lovely Mum also got me interested in having a few sips of Irish whisky with cream. This great combination (in moderation of course) helped to revive my circulation tremendously.

The benefits of drinking moderate amounts of red wine have been well documented, particularly with people who have high cholesterol and, as mentioned before, it's recommended by some doctors for patients recovering from heart surgery. If you ever do have a few glasses too many, make sure you have a day between, drinking plenty of water to give your system a detox before having another day with any alcohol consumption.

Information supplied by the National Health Service in the U.K. suggests that the recommended total of alcohol units for women per day is below 2-3 units (with two alcohol free days per week) and for men is below 3-4 units per day (with two alcohol free days per week).

1 pint of beer or larger (4% abv) 2.3 units
1 pint of cider or export larger (5% abv) 2.8 units
1 glass of wine 175ml (12% abv) 2.3 units
1 single measure of spirits (40% abv) 1 unit

abv = alcohol by volume

Preventing Self-abuse

To prevent self-abuse by using drugs, excess alcohol by over or under eating, or even practicing excessive exercise is to ask yourself 'if a child came to you feeling anxious, upset or worried would you force feed them drugs, alcohol or food, or starve them, or make them run on a treadmill to make them feel better? Or would you give them reassurance, a little treat and your love?'

The child in *your* care is your 'inner child' within you. Take your inner child out to play, change the subject and nourish your soul with fun and laughter as often as possible to maintain 'balance' in your life.

Another top tip if you've been taking an anti-biotic, or have had a bit too much alcohol or if you simply feel a bit run down is to take some drinks or yoghurts that contain pre and pro-biotic bacteria to replace the friendly bacteria in your system and to give your system a boost. I suggest you only take these supplements for a few days to help you regain balance.

Awareness of Your Metabolic Rate in Recovery

When we are asleep our bodies reach a stage where they function on what is termed as our BASAL METABOLIC RATE (BMR). This is when the minimum amount of energy is expended by the body to maintain our vital processes e.g. respiration, circulation and digestion. It's expressed medically in terms of heat production per unit of body surface area per day and various factors such as age, sex and particularly thyroid activity influence the value of our BMR.

Eating an evening meal early is important so that your food can be fully digested before you wake up the next morning, giving your body important time to rest in the BMR state and allowing maximum rest.

When food passes from our stomach into our intestines, muscular movements called *peristalsis* take place. These are involuntary actions of the intestines, which we have no control over. If you imagine your intestines as a rubber tube for a moment, place two small balls into the imaginary tube to represent balls of food passing through your intestine. Now imagine your hands squeezing the tube so the balls are moved from one end to the other. Your hands represent the internal muscles of the intestines. That's how the action of peristalsis works. Although an involuntary movement, it's enhanced by bodily movement, which is why it's important to watch your diet and it's good to get moving. If you're really relaxed and lying on a bed and very gentle and patient with yourself and place your hand just under you're tummy button area you can sometimes even *feel* the movement of peristalsis happening!

Fasting has been well known for centuries to help cleanse and rest the body at intervals and is even thought to be a factor in aiding longevity. However, whilst recovering from and coping with any form of illness I wouldn't personally recommend fasting but *awareness* I highly recommend! It's important to be aware of what happens with regard to our BMR whilst we sleep so we can assist and achieve optimum rest.

It's estimated that a large percentage of us are all, at some stage, suffering from a degree of sleep depravation which in turn directly affects our metabolism. Our *eyesight* is greatly affected by tiredness. Our sight becomes affected with sometimes the slightest tiredness and illness, can differ throughout the day, and is greatly affected by our blood sugar levels. Even a change in the weather can affect our sight. An examination or two at the opticians is a great way of keeping a check on things: but I suggest you get a good night's sleep and make sure you've eaten beforehand. (I've included some yogic eye exercises later on in the book in the 'How to *Thrive* in the Workplace' section to help keep your eyes limbered up and functioning favourably!).

Taking 'Time Out' - the Choice is Ours

Sometimes it becomes absolutely necessary to listen to the 'voice within' to free our spirit from restriction and do exactly whatever our heart is telling us to do. So long as it isn't a danger to others we should go for it, without restriction!

If we're in disharmony our mind or body will be showing us in one or possibly a number of areas in our life. Through observation of our thoughts and by changing their direction during times of peace and time out just to 'be', we're able to observe what our mind, body and spirit is telling us. One of the main things I want to bring awareness to is that when we look into it, in most aspects of our lives, it's possible to realise and remember that we *do* have choices. We can't control natural disasters, but our life structure, our ways of dealing with situations and our lifestyle can be controlled.

To an enormous extent with a different approach we can change things in our lives. We do have choice; our own mind is our only limitation.

Each day provides new challenges and it's entirely up to us what we do with our day. For instance, if you have a job and decide that you need to stay off work for a day to preserve your sanity - so be it! Or if you wish to go up to the top of a hill, look at the view, contemplate life and do some problem solving for a short while, you have the freedom of choice to do just that. You most likely won't automatically lose your job and you'll be doing yourself a huge favour by learning a greater understanding of your needs and desires! You'll be able to refresh yourself from the inside out, breathe fresh air into your body and be brighter eyed and bushier tailed ready for work the next day and your employers will benefit too.

Taking time off regularly helps us to regain balance in our lives. Sounds simple? Check out when you last took time out. Planning a few long weekends and holidays whenever possible (especially if you're working) helps to relieve stress and fatigue. You don't have to spend money, just a nice long day out walking in the country or going to a park can work wonders!

Whatever the circumstances it's important that we occasionally release some of our commitments, free ourselves and make way for new energies to enter our lives. By letting a few of the balls we are juggling fall to the wayside, we can re-focus and feel that we don't need to live up to other's needs and expectations.

Listening to our bodies is a natural art. It's healthy and fair for us to take time out, pace ourselves and set out our individual patterns of rest, relaxation and exercise. You don't have to stick to my times exactly. In fact you'll feel more in control when you work out your own patterns and you'll get to know your own body rhythms more than ever before and see your progress for yourself.

Suggestion snippets:

- To broaden our knowledge is always a healthy way to keep our minds active and balanced. Adult evening courses at college or Open University can be a great way to try out new things and some courses also offer qualifications which can lead to new opportunities.

- Voluntary work is a great way of helping out in the community and also a good way to get out of the house and meet new people. Occasionally it can even also lead to future employment opportunities.

- Joining clubs is a good way to meet 'like minded' people and many relationships and friendships can blossom from this:

You could try adding another string to your bow and do something you haven't done before. Like archery or flower arranging, for girls and boys! 'This' is an ideal time, even if you just peruse the brochures.

The wheel of life is thankfully forever changing ~ live each and 'every moment' to the full.

Housework and Chores

This was one of my most popular areas of discussion with friends and family whilst recovering from M.E./ C.F.S. and still is to this day! A great practice to get into is to spread chores out and break them down into manageable pieces. Over time it can make a remarkable difference to your energy levels.

Research has shown even just after 90 minutes or so of time our body cells need replenishing. No matter what our lifestyle, or what we're doing, it's important to take regular breaks of 10 to 15 minutes every so often to lessen strain on our bodies. By momentarily shutting out the world, we can simply re-focus for a while on just a calm breathing pattern (ideal time for a short relaxation or meditation see the 'Mini-Holiday' meditation in a further chapter). It's good to allow 15 minutes so you have sufficient time to come around afterwards before you begin the next task. Regular practice of this can go a long way to replenishing our energy levels and also keeping our thoughts positive and spirits high.

Many of us feel we should always be *'doing'* instead of just *'being',* what's the urgency? Do yourself a favour and literally lengthen your life expectancy by trying not to fuel situations with a sense of urgency unless it really is an emergency!

I know this may sound like common sense, but it's surprising how we tend to lose sight of this, particularly when we're stressed, depressed or unwell. Maybe you could look into the possibility of getting some help with the shopping, housework and gardening until you feel better, especially if you live alone. Of course, if you live with someone else, ask for as much help as possible. Is there a neighbour or friend that can help? It's still important, however, to try to be able to do some chores and cooking yourself to keep active, involved and independent.

Because stress and illness affects every area of our life here are a few tips regarding shopping to help save your energy so you can put it towards your recovery instead.

- First ask yourself is your shopping urgently needed today or can you use up what you have in the cupboard and shop tomorrow? A good store of dried pasta, rice, tins of beans, spaghetti, macaroni cheese, tomatoes, some dried cheese powder, eggs, bacon and ham are always great to fall back on. When tomorrow comes do just a little shopping at a time instead of taking on a big shopping spree out of fear of running out.

- Internet shopping is the ideal way to take the strain out of shopping as goods can be delivered directly to your door. There must be a neighbour or friend who would be willing to help out with the ordering, all that's needed from you is a list and payment.

- Many of us, myself included, get into the habit of overbuying food, particularly if there's a bank holiday coming up. Have you ever noticed how the supermarkets are crammed with people panic buying? It's a good habit to ask yourself if you really need items of shopping, food or otherwise, before you decide to buy.

- With regard to food, I suggest you try to plan a seven-day menu ahead but don't worry if you can't manage to do this at first.

Housework

- With regard to housework, if you don't have anyone to help you, it's worth hiring a housekeeper to give a thorough spring clean so all that's needed is a small amount of maintenance.

- Break your housework time down and do tasks in small stages. For example, if changing bed linen, after you have removed the linen for cleaning rest for ten minutes before replacing your fresh linen. Rest again and then do the dusting. Take a further rest time, then do the vacuuming and so on. Practice of this can help to make tasks more manageable, which in-turn is good for helping to raise your self- esteem.

- With regard to gardening, you could find out if there's a helpful neighbour who'll help with the lawns or hire a garden contractor and get them to cut hedges back a little more drastically than usual so they won't need so much care for a while. Keeping a few patio pots can brighten things up and give a stunning all year round display and helps you to stay active and productive!

Suggestions to break down chores at home:

After breakfast sit down and prepare your vegetables for the day's meals, even if you do one lot then rest and go back to them later (once others heard about this method, they never looked back!). Prepare root vegetables as and when required to prevent dehydration. Preparing meals in stages allows you to conserve your energy. Depending on how your condition/metabolism affects you, simply adjust the timing to suit you as an individual and the lifestyle you have.

- A great way to stimulate and balance both sides of your body is to do housework using both your left and right hands; it exercises and evens out muscle tone and nerve responses.

- Make a song and dance of housework - try listening to your favourite CD and groove while

Elizabeth Bailey

> you move to banish boredom and stimulate
> your senses!

Once you adjust to regular patterns of activity and rest
it's possible to increase your energy levels greatly ~
remember the stairway to healing! You may have set
backs but these are to be expected and are all part of
the healing process.

Onward and upward! ~ Keep moving forward.

Try to do things just one step at a time.

Toxic Awareness

You may not like to know this, but it's an important fact with regard to *healing,* that you should be aware of the toxins in our environment and how they can affect us. Many synthetic chemicals have been linked to illnesses and conditions and we really can't be sure what effect this cocktail of chemicals will have on any forms of life on this planet in the long term.

Many toxins can be found in manmade chemicals used daily in our homes. The safest option is to use cleaning products, cosmetics and toiletries that contain non-toxic ingredients and are made from natural ingredients. Thankfully, there are now many companies who are manufacturing these products made with natural plant based ingredients that are safer for our environment and us. The way *forward* is *awareness* coupled with the growing *demand* for cleaning products and toiletries to contain only non-toxic, plant based ingredients which are safer for us and for our aquatic life.

It's a fact that 40% of what we put on our skin or hair is absorbed into our bloodstream. This can cause harmful side effects to our health, indeed there are claims that many illnesses including M.E./C.F.S. have been cleared up by simply changing to naturally produced products containing no harsh chemicals which can have a toxic effect and can be the cause of many symptoms. Some chemicals, which are widely used in most toiletries, can cause such symptoms as headaches and lethargy and can damage our bodies at cellular level, which we may not be aware of, particularly if toiletries are used in any quantity over the above-recommended amounts.

It's also important to be aware that inhaled aerosol ingredients penetrate into lungs and the bloodstream and talcum powder once inhaled never leaves our bodies. Also that many air fresheners carry a chemical which literally deadens our smell receptors. In positive, *heavenly* contrast, just a dab or two of pure natural aromatherapy oil on a tissue in a room or placed on a radiator can make a room smell sweetly scented and have added health benefits too.

When using the essences for room fragrance a few drops of pure essential oil onto a tissue placed into a saucer of water and placed on top of a radiator makes an effective vaporiser, or alternatively, rub a drop of the oil onto a cold light bulb (but remember to unplug from electricity socket first). When the bulb warms up you can enjoy the natural aroma of nature's finest oils.

Our skin is a living and breathing system just as our lungs are.

Our sense of smell is one of the most powerful of our senses and one of our first senses we are aware of at birth. Factually, it is also the last to leave us. Thousands of years ago our ancestors used aromatic herbs and resins with knowledge of their beneficial effects. In 3500BC the priestesses of the Egyptian temples were burning frankincense to clear the mind and the Romans used aromatic herbs and essential oils widely for massage and in the home.

The great herbalist Dr Culpepper used such oils, particularly rosemary and peppermint as an integral part of his medicine and was able to investigate herbal remedies for many ailments taking an awareness of the benefits of herbalism to a new stratosphere of knowledge for us.

As well as being absorbent, our skin breathes and is one of our major detox systems. Toxins, including excess alcohol are released through our skin. By cleaning it regularly and gently scrubbing away old skin cells, we wash away not just dirt and bacteria, but toxins too.

During my journey of recovery, one of the subjects that I wanted to become more attuned to was the subject of 'de-toxifying the body'. For some time now there's been controversy about the link of amalgam fillings in our teeth being possibly linked to illnesses, one of them being M.E./C.F.S. I've since found out that the actual practice of removing fillings greatly *increases* the dangers of exposing the body to more amalgam/mercury, so it's seems to be safer to leave them where they are and replace them with fillings which don't contain mercury, as and when they deteriorate. There is, however, evidence that removal of fillings can have a remarkable effect on health and there are dentists who perform routine removal of mercury fillings should that be your choice.

Luckily, my Son and I we were able to recover to such a remarkable degree that tooth fillings, I concluded, could not be the *cause* of our particular condition.

Tips to help detoxify

- It's good for your skin to go without make up or creams now and again. Even some moisturisers can have a suffocating effect on our skin. Letting your skin *breathe* avoids the plastic bag effect of skin asphyxiation.

- A gentle reminder - remember to drink more water then drink a bit more again. Not only do we expel water vapour through our obvious trips to the bathroom, we also lose water via our skin and through our breath and perspiration. We need to constantly top up our water levels at every opportunity to maintain a healthy balance.

- A walk in the rain or by the sea is a wonderful way to naturally moisturise and refresh your skin – nature's spritzer!

- Try to seek out natural cleaning products for your home. Most major supermarkets and good chemist shops now sell products which are naturally based, are safe to use and don't harm the environment as other harsh chemicals most definitely do - and *demand* will prevail!

- Avoid foods, which contain additives – look out for natural products.

- Try to avoid using a microwave.

- A great way to boost the body's immune system is to get good daily supplies of vitamins and minerals in fresh foods:

- Beta-carotene, and particularly vitamins B complex, C, E and selenium, help to fight the dangers of pollutants in the body and our exposure to free radicals.

  These essential vitamins and minerals can be found in all fresh fruit and vegetables, wholewheat flour and rice, eggs, cheese, meat and fish.

How to 'Thrive' in the Work place

Times of illness and taking time out due to stress can be ideal times to listen to your heart and find the work you *love and enjoy.* To live a life and have very few regrets about what you wish you had of done is what fulfilment is about. Factually, the majority of us spend most of our lives working, therefore it makes simple sense to be happy in our work. Following our heart's desires takes enormous courage, yet by following our hearts instead of being restricted by our heads, particularly when it comes to work, can have a profoundly positive effect on our health and well-being.

However your condition affects you, if you are returning to work, as well as being aware of how to pace yourself and use your time wisely, it's important to know the facts on legal lengths of time between breaks and how sitting at a computer screen, if you have one, may affect you.

A subject that's very close to my heart is that to my mind we *all* need to readjust our working and rest patterns, particularly in the workplace, to live healthier and longer lives.

Suggestions to cover at work:

- Talk to your employer about your condition concentrating on your *positive strengths.* Like family, your employers also need to be told that you're unwell, but you are getting better and need to simply stick to regular break times. Try to include a ten-minute break at least every two hours to just sit quietly away from your working environment and to *refuel* with food and drink.

- Make sure you drink every hour and a half and that you eat something every three hours.

- Be firm with yourself. Don't feel guilty in any way about taking your breaks.

- Remember that our health is the most important investment we can make. Your employer can work out for themselves if they want to introduce a rule to include everyone else. I guarantee firms would have far less absence if they looked at their employee's welfare more positively and implemented 'healthier' working conditions.

- Never push yourself. Always 'P A C E'. Organise and delegate out as much as possible, in the nicest possible way of course!

- It can be beneficial to have a small routine the evening before work to prepare everything you need for the following day ahead. You can plan what you'll have for lunch at work and take perfect energy snacks like fresh fruits, raisins, rice cakes with luscious and nutritious toppings like, butter (naughty but nice), turkey breast and cranberry jelly, or pots of cooked pasta or rice and chopped cucumber, tomatoes, prawns, peas and fresh mayonnaise (just add mayonnaise in the morning).

- Don't settle for second best when it comes to drinks at work. Bring your own organic tea bags and drinks and always sip water throughout the day to keep your mind and body alert and hydrated.

- Make sure you have a walk about, especially at lunchtime. Go out in the fresh air if possible to get re-oxygenated and help to *naturally* de-stress yourself.

- Regular breaks are not 'just' breaks, they are essential to your health and well-being and should also be maintained throughout your life, whether you're working or not.

- Exercise your muscles including your heart muscle by taking the stairs instead of the lift if you have one.

- Do your eyes a favour and get away from close work and walk about and stretch your body out.

- It's estimated that if you work at a computer screen you should have a twenty minute break away from the computer every hour.

To soothe and relax tired eyes rub your palms together until they feel warm then cup your hands over your eyes for a minute or two without pressure and let the natural warmth and darkness soothe away any tension.

If you work in a busy environment where the telephone constantly rings, before answering it immediately, take a good slow deep breath in and out to balance your energy levels and counteract stress. Work this into all situations in your life, whenever you start to feel under pressure. Along with decent regular breaks and walks, this helps us (just like releasing the lid of a pressure cooker) to let off a bit of steam!

If you work on a keyboard here's a good exercise to help to avoid repetitive strain injury. Make sure you've got plenty of room in front of you. Place your arms out at full length and shoulder height in front of you, with palms facing downward. Check that your shoulders are relaxed and breathe in slowly and deeply through your nose. As you slowly breathe out make a gentle fist with your fingers. Repeat this five times at least every hour or so to build strength in your fingers, hands, wrists and shoulders and to lubricate your joints.

To ease shoulder strain sit correctly with your spine upright, so that your posture is comfortable and at ease (ensuring that your feet are placed flat on the floor and that your knees are bent without strain). Check how your body feels, right up to your head, rotate your shoulders forward three times then back slowly three times to release any tension. Then gently raise and lower both of your shoulders at the same time three times.

To ease stress throughout the day check frequently that your posture is comfortable and at ease.

To release tension in your neck sit comfortably with your spine straight. Very gently now and again move your head slowly to the right, back to the centre and slowly to the left. Then tip your chin down towards your chest, then back to the centre before slowly and very gently, tipping your head backwards. Chin up!

If you work at a computer screen, in particular, make sure you drink plenty of water to keep hydrated and to maintain concentration and energy levels.

Eye Exercises

Practice of regular daily eye exercises can prolong good eyesight and weak eyesight can be improved. Eye exercises strengthen the muscles behind the eyes and can also improve your concentration.

To avoid eyestrain particularly when working at a computer screen and when you're reading (when your eyes continuously focus and re-focus at the same distance) it's good to exercise your eye muscles by occasionally looking away and into the distance.

A good yogic eye exercise to increase strength in your eye muscles and improve sight is to sit in a straight-backed chair or crossed legged comfortable on the floor. Keep your feet flat on the ground. Relax one hand on your lap. Then with your arm out at full length turn your hand so your palm is facing upward and hold your index finger up in front of you at eye level.

1. First look at the tip of your finger. Then look past your finger and into the distance so that your finger goes into 'soft focus' then focus back on to the finger. Repeat this five times then close your eyes for a moment and rest.

2. Repeat with the other index finger extended at arm's length and eye level.

3. Repeat the sequence by closing one eye.

4. Repeat by closing the other eye, and close your eyes to rest.

Elizabeth Bailey

Horizontal and Vertical Eye Exercise

1. Simply rest your hands in your lap and keep your head still and facing forward.

2. Look to the right and back to the centre. Then to the left and back to the centre. Repeat this five times to each side.

3. Then look up without moving your head and back to the centre. Then look down and then back to the centre. Repeating this five times. Then close your eyes and rest for a moment.

Take the Stress out of Driving

A tip for everyone in the world who drives. If you want to feel less stressed make more time for car journeys and practice driving slower than you have done in the past. Needless to say never exceed speed limits but go very slightly slower ~ *try it and see!*

- Getting someone else to drive at every opportunity can help to preserve our energy levels and taking turns to drive can be of benefit to all concerned particularly when going on long journeys.

Holidays

- Try to take regular holidays whether working or not.

- Factually after being away from work or anywhere for 2 days we only then begin to start to wind down. When we are away from our home environment our bodies don't entirely wind down until the 'fourth day'. However, by practicing the art of regular relaxation and meditation our bodies are able to adjust to relaxation faster.

A fantastic way for you to wind down is to practice the habit of simply sitting quietly for a moment or two when you come in from work.

For example turn your mobile off, close the curtains, light a candle and simply just 'be' for 10 minutes. That's all it takes to ground yourself again. Remember that daily practice is the key. Simply close your eyes and breathe in through your nose slowly, filling your lungs comfortably. Imagine being showered with golden light from above, filling you with positive thoughts and energy. Then on an 'out' breath, release all tension, negative thoughts and tiredness. Repeat this for three breaths. It can help to calm and re-focus your thoughts.

Stilling the mind with peace for just *one minute* in meditation and focussing on your breath with your eyes closed can re-new your energy, re-build your body, calm your emotions and re-shape your thoughts to release great reserves of strength and power.

We all have a certain amount of energy, *our life force*. If we burn it away and deplete our energy through overwork or excess in our lives, our bodies will oblige us, to a point. It's always necessary to restore this energy and this is what is known as 'balance'.

It's a fact: rushing gets us nowhere fast in life!

The Power of Positive Thought

No matter who we are or how much or how little wealth we have, life is always a mixture of positives and negatives. There are different types of issues we face on a daily basis and if the matter is something that's within our power to do something about it's up to our individual choice whether we approach them with a positive or negative mental attitude.

If we recognise that our thoughts and energies are going towards something we have no real control over, by 'letting go' of intense thoughts, we automatically free up the flow of our energy and make way for new constructive energy to flow, giving us precious time to get on with our lives in a positive way for ourselves with fantastic results!

Some of the hardest battles we encounter are in our own minds. With constant and persistent reminders of *'positive'* thoughts we can change our own thought patterns to a remarkable degree. This important process can help to both empower and heal our lives.

- Thought is a specific force in nature, our thoughts continuously bring about changes in our physical body and our personal thoughts also affect our environment and our associates. It's a scientific fact that negative, erratic thought processes drain the body and indeed the mind of energies and that positive thoughts have a remarkable effect on our energy levels. Positive thought process helps us to recognise spirals of negativity when they start to arise.

- It's easy to for us to waste vital energy on complaining about things, instead try transforming negativity into creative *'action'*. It's easy to say and simple to understand, but *practice* is the key.

- By practicing positive thinking, your body and mind will 'thrive', as positive thoughts enhance feelings of pleasure in your brain. Once that pattern is recognised and practiced your brain won't want to go back to negative thinking!

- Try to analyse your thoughts, yes all of them, and whenever a negative thought comes into your mind, counterbalance it with a positive one. Eventually, the positive pattern takes over, it's scientifically proven to be energy producing, incredibly uplifting and, furthermore, practising positive thoughts is also contagious! With practice, you'll be coming up with a positive answer to almost *everything*. It takes practice, but it works and most definitely, positive thoughts about your healing will help to speed your recovery.

- Scientific tests prove that positive thinking can also build our resistance when it comes to fighting illness and pain.

- Positive energy is everywhere in our bodies and around us in forms of electrically charged positive and negative ions. Try to visit the sea and charge up with the natural healing ions of the ocean.

- Just as we should learn to practice positive thinking it's healthy to also acknowledge releasing anger, emotion or tension to help us to re- balance. Holding onto negative feelings can be damaging and can manifest as physical problems if ignored. Anger and hatred can lead to revenge and become self-destructive. Taking control of our own minds is vital to our well-being. The process of writing our thoughts down or screaming into a pillow or going for a brisk walk can be good safe ways to help to release anger or tension.

Factually, a certain amount of stress in our lives helps to keep us performing at our best. We're designed for healthy challenges to help keep our minds sharp and our bodies firing on all cylinders! Having something to strive for is part of nature.

After we've done our very best in situations and feel we can do no more it's good to learn to let go of worries and unburden ourselves by letting it all go out to the Universe or our God/the Angels. Look up to the sky and ask for guidance, say it out loud or write your concerns or worries down on a small piece of paper then burn them safely. Guidance can also be asked for whenever we pray. By saying or sending our thoughts out and asking for guidance, we learn to release ourselves from burden and let nature take its course.

It's incredible then, how things can come back to us with positive results. These methods of releasing literally free up our energy to then be able to focus ourselves in a more positive direction.

Why do we ever give away our personal power and let another being or situation demand all our attention and energy? *We have choices....*

It's a fact that positive thinking broadens our outlook and more positive things start to happen in our lives.

Problem Solving

A good tip if ever you're facing problems of any kind and to help put things into perspective is to first remind yourself that everyone, including yourself, is on his or her own journey in life. Problems that arise can then be placed easier into categories and situations can often be diffused.

The practice of problem solving can bring about astonishing levels of positive thinking, it's therapeutic and everyone around you will notice especially when you start to sing regularly. Which is a fantastic sign of positivity!

Try to only tackle matters a few minutes at a time then leave what you're doing and take a break, or better still go for a walk in the fresh air for 15 minutes to get your endorphins going again. If it's an unresolved matter after 15 minutes and it can't wait until another day then return to it and think of the most 'positive' brain storming solution you can.

Again, the process of writing things down or even saying them to yourself can help to resolve matters:

- Firstly, write down what the problem or challenge is at the top of a   page

- Then what you wish from the outcome

- Then list at least three or more brainstorming solutions that you can think of that could help resolve the situation

- List the pros and cons of the brainstorming solution you choose

- Then write down your decision of the best action to take

- Then what action is required for you to make that happen

- Make sure you try to follow it up by listing the outcome of what happened

Another good way to approach a problem is to imagine a friend has come to you with your problem. Either say the problem to yourself and answer as a friend or write it down and reply with the best possible intent for that person.

Time Out and Task Management

- A way to make sure you are looking after yourself and to also manage your time on tasks is to make a list with two headings of 'time out' and 'tasks'. Firstly, list things to do to treat yourself then list any tasks that may need doing on that day. Secondly, list what you're going to do for yourself the following day and any task that needs doing. Then record what you are going to do for yourself that week, that month and so on. With the tasks, prioritise each one but keep your 'me time' always as top priority. Try to make the task list as simple as possible to avoid any extra pressure. It's surprising how by simply doing this you can achieve more. It can also alleviate feelings of pressure and in addition help to raise your self-esteem.

- Take the fear out of finances. Allow only ten minutes at a time on sorting out any financial matters. Money is a form of energy. Like all energies it requires balance. The less we need or want anything in life, when we let go of the wanting and needing and put our energy into positive action, the more positive results come back to us.

Try to counter balance your life with times of leisure and pure pleasure between all tasks. As well as energy producing, it's also an excellent way of coping with depression.

Raising Self-Esteem

If you're suffering from low self-esteem and lack of motivation don't doubt yourself any longer. Take a stand and stop beating yourself up inside. Be proud of yourself no matter what you have been previously *programmed* to believe about yourself by others or even by yourself.

- Affirm to yourself the following affirmation, saying it out loud or in your mind, three times:

'I am an immaculate creation of the Universe inside and out.
My self-respect is high. I am strong, I am in control.
I am intuitive and happy to be me'

Learning to take a stand calmly but firmly in your own beliefs helps to raise self-esteem and if anyone tries to fill you with doubt tell them politely to back off!

To boost self-esteem try not to beat yourself up mentally or physically. Being humans we do tend to do this rather a lot. If ever you are feeling a bit low:

- Try looking into a mirror then say out loud how you feel about yourself.

- Ask yourself if you would say the same things to a friend or anyone for that matter. If it's all 'good' things and compliments, keep it going! But if it would be unacceptable for you to be saying them to someone else, then why are you saying them to yourself?

- Remind yourself of someone in your life who loves or has loved you, it could even be a pet. Think about the love they gave you. Love is always there, you don't have to be with that person to feel love for them. Love can be in thought and goes on forever. Love yourself as they did and *still do.*

- Affirm to yourself that, no matter what, you are a special, unique human being and that you are loved (by yourself) and others past or present. Repeat this as often as you can.

- Correct any 'negative illusions' you may have and raise your self-esteem. It's totally within 'your' power. You can begin a new lifestyle right now!

- If ever you catch yourself putting yourself down in any way, it's good to follow up what you have said or thought with a positive remark about yourself. With practice, this can have a great effect on raising your confidence and boosting your self-esteem.

Write down and compliment yourself on all your attributes as regularly as possible.

- Our bad moods are always a good sign to get ourselves out and about, change the subject and feed our inner self's needs with pleasurable activity. We can all get engrossed with our own concerns at times and when we begin to recognise our 'triggers' to stress, the sooner we can deal with them and make our lives less serious and predictable, the better and healthier we become.

'Feel good' suggestions:

- Doing things on the spur of the moment can be exhilarating! Pushing through comfort zones and not resisting change can bring about wonderful opportunities. I've tried it out often with many of my clients, family and friends with *great* results. Do something totally different and see how you feel afterwards, it can also be great for beating depression. Simply stop everything else and treat yourself to enormous portions of fun!

Elizabeth Bailey

- Listening to the laughter of children at play can remind us that it's ok and our given right to relax, have fun and be happy. No matter what age you are, take your inner self out to play, have a break and some fun. Take yourself out whenever you can to the cinema, the theatre (pantomimes can be great fun for all ages) take a boat trip or visit the circus or zoo to nourish your soul.

- Crying is O.K. and it's been scientifically proven. Crying prompts our body to release 'feel good hormones' to maintain homeostasis, so as long as it doesn't become too invasive or occur too regularly, it's best not to bottle your emotions up and just go with the flow.

- We often get fixed into taking up certain roles and images in life such as partner, employee, carer, mother, father, grandmother or grandfather etc. and we can sometimes forget who we really are inside. It's important for our health and well-being to be able to know and address what our 'needs' and 'desires' are to enable us to feel whole again. Taking regular time out of our roles helps us to regain control of who we are.

- Try not to let suffering consume your whole being. Give yourself all the time you need, especially when it comes to healing. Sometimes we need to go through suffering to be able to heal and regain balance in our lives. Try to be

156

patient with yourself and give yourself time to gain strength and to heal.

- Let's talk about it. Undoubtedly there's something very therapeutic about the fantastic healing value of being able to voice ourselves. Being able to talk of our thoughts and the act of speaking about matters can be so beneficial. When we come to vocalise our thoughts, fears or worries, they begin to take on new meaning.

Professional counselling can enable you to eventually get to a point where you're actually fed up with talking about your worries. What's important is that it doesn't matter how long it takes, it's all part of the healing process. If you do decide to take this route, I suggest you track down a good counsellor. They are of course, all totally individual, it's great then to find one who you can 'connect' with and there *will* be one out there who will be 'just right' for you.

Get that feel good factor functioning!

It's been scientifically proven that by looking at pleasant pictures or being out doors in the beautiful surroundings of nature causes an increase of blood flow to the pleasure areas of our brain. This causes fantastic chemical reactions within us and we release an abundance of feel good hormones.

- Try to surround yourself as much as possible with beautiful pictures of nature. The human body form is also stunning and beautiful both in sculpture and picture form.

- Take time to daydream, visualise and explore new places as much as you can. Too much work on any matter is drudgery!

- Talking of riches, as we all know they don't bring us inner happiness. Only you can do that. Having high standards in life is no sin and I'm sure the Universe would also agree that no one is more spiritual if they have less possessions. In truth we are all equal.

- Simple, free treats like watching sunsets and sleeping under the stars out of love for oneself can work wonders to revive the soul.

- Try taking a steam train ride, it's so relaxing, like having a full body massage at cellular level!

The present is just that - a gift.

Balancing Relationships

One of the things that struck me whilst working as a therapist and even more so recently, is the importance of the health of our relationships. It's certainly one of life's hardest lessons to learn and a subject that is so important to cover. No matter what, it's healthy to have our own 'scared space' within all relationships we come across.

We all have bad times as well as good and they can often lead us to find our correct paths in life. Though it may seem heartbreaking at the time, we are sometimes forced to make changes, particularly if we find ourselves in a destructive relationship, if we are unhappy in our job, or when we find that a friendship is untrustworthy. We may still be better off out of that particular situation. After all, the danger has passed and we are able to move on to a brighter future, which may be infinitely more suitable for us.

We are all one humanity and there are some evil people out there, but thankfully, there's still a million times more good than evil in this world and we all have a choice of which path we decide to take, good, bad or indifferent. We learn through our experiences and from *each other.*

If we burden our minds with responsibilities of our own or others we lose touch with our own creativity and inspiration, yet, when we start to take time out we can begin to rediscover our own 'truths' which can have a positive effect on everyone around us.

Some of our major stresses are directly linked to our environments and involve partners, family and friends. If you're living with or around people it's good to take time out to get away from your usual environment regularly to clear your mind. Having precious time alone can help to take some of the stress out of your life. We don't own others and they don't own us. Go it alone sometimes and watch the benefits! Don't forget to encourage your family member, work colleague or partner to do the same on his or her own giving you both valuable time to yourselves and bringing about a healthy balance all round.

With regard to wedded bliss it's a fact that many happily married couples do live longer having loving relationships. Generally, these partnerships have a 'healthy balance' and they are couples who show each other the unconditional love that is the sole basis of true love itself.

It's up to us not to allow ourselves to become too absorbed by other people's problems and the drama that can surround them, particularly if it's being directed at us. It's good to remind ourselves sometimes that we can't possibly deal with everything that comes our way in life (unless, of course, we possess superhuman powers!). It's OK to just sit back sometimes when we've done our best and simply 'let go'.

As I've already mentioned, our living environment has an incredible effect on our health and having a stable, happy home life contributes to our well-being enormously. When feeling stressed or unwell, it's all too easy to isolate ourselves with our feelings, so it's good to get out into the fresh air as soon as you feel up to it. Explore nature, observe its beauty, holiness and the power of which we are all a part.

It's good to value your friends and family. When we're out of sorts it's easy to lose touch with ourselves and snap at others around us. People don't always understand that it's because we are unwell, that we are temporarily 'not ourselves'. If people around you have been supportive, give back to them by thanking them, it costs nothing but it means so much to be thanked. Imagine for a moment how things are from their point of view. It's easy to forget how much it means to receive thanks. Practice by giving a smile, a compliment and ask how they are too. Giving thanks can be healing for everyone.

It's necessary to remind ourselves often that we are totally in control of our own lives. If we feel we aren't, it's because we are letting someone or something else call the shots!

No one can posses you unless you believe they can.

Essential Love and Hugs

As fundamental as breathing, eating or sleeping, we need to experience the many different forms of love in our lives. Experiencing love is just as important to our lives than any other matter of our being. Love can have a profound effect on our energy levels and immune system and *giving* love is just as important as *receiving* it.

When we express love it can have a dramatic effect on our emotions, health and well-being. Love is one of the most powerful, strangest and certainly strongest of all forces in our known Universe, as anyone who has ever been 'truly' in love will agree.

Love comes in many forms. You may be sceptical about the benefits of complementary therapies and support groups, but there's no doubt that patients who've been diagnosed with terminal illnesses have lived for longer through attending support groups and their suffering is lessened when acceptance, love and peace are found.

By finding love within yourself and addressing your *own* needs it's possible to heal in so many ways. People without self-love in their lives often abuse themselves through alcohol or drug-abuse, or even overeating to compensate for lack of love. When it comes to relationships with partners *too much* dependency is usually a sign of fear in disguise and through loving one's self and being at one, relationships that happen naturally, without force, are meaningful and comparatively trouble free in contrast.

Like many things in life it's the *quality* not the *quantity* of love that counts. We could have an abundance of low quality love given to us, but nothing equals the infinite power of unconditional love we can have for ourselves. Love doesn't have to be that we are physically with a person to experience feelings of love. It can be in thoughts and in spirit. Because someone may have left this spiritual plane doesn't mean that their love is gone, love lasts forever in spirit and *loving memories* prove that.

There's a deep spiritual hunger in many of us at times and awareness is the key. When we are able to be open enough we can adjust our lifestyles to include the many forms of the essential healing power of *love* in our lives.

Laughter, love, life – so precious

- Love can directly affect your immune system. It's been scientifically proven that people with happy love lives suffer less from viral infections such as colds and flu.

- Accept nothing but the best for yourself when it comes to love. Buy yourself a gift at Christmas or better still, anytime that you can afford it!

- When we begin to love ourselves we find inner peace, a sense of calm and a better understanding of ourselves and everyone around us.

- It's a proven fact that the act of making love has a greater medicinal benefit to the body, mind and spirit than any other medical drug known!

TRUE LOVE COMES FROM WITHIN
The answer to any problem is love.

The Power of Affirmations

Affirmations can have an enormously positive impact on our thoughts and well-being and can be used in all situations to gain balance and harmony.

In stressful situations or if your trust, pride or security has been threatened, take time to be still. Close your eyes and as you breathe in think of the following words:

Breathe in to the words and sounds of: *I am full of peace*

Breathe out to the words:*I am full of harmony*

Keep repeating this until you feel more peaceful.

You can make up your own affirmations to suit your day. Inspirational, positive words and sentences said to yourself will encourage balance and harmony. Here are just a few examples:

Try saying to yourself momentarily throughout your day from the start to its end one or more of the following three times:

- I do not waste my energies on useless worry.

- I look upon all challenges as opportunities.

- One minute of anger is 60 seconds of unhappiness.

- I am positive and dynamic.

- I am true to myself, because I am worth it.

- I love myself, maintain perfect health and don't waste my energies with worry about others thoughts and actions.

- I feel no fear, I feel no fear, I feel no fear, (try writing this down to enforce it's meaning and your strength).

Writing affirmations down on notepaper and placing them on your refrigerator door, mirror or computer, is a great way to remind yourself to repeat them in your mind or out loud throughout the day.

Affirmation Meditation

Find a quiet place where you are not going to be disturbed.

Stand or sit with your spine straight (without strain).

Lightly touch each thumb with your index finger forming a gentle curl of your finger and thumb (this has been used for centuries in the eastern part of the world to re-circulate energy and focus the mind).

Close your eyes, take a slow deep breath in through your nose feeling your diaphragm expand and release the breath slowly. Become aware of how your body is feeling from head to toe. By bringing awareness to any areas that may have tension you are able to help to free up these areas.

Take a few moments to be still and say a favourite affirmation within to your mind, body and emotions.

Natural strength, power, peace and the fullness of love are within us all.

Complimentary Healing Methods

It's not the healer who has magical powers, it's how your own body and mind heal within yourself as a whole. We are 'all' unique creations of the Universe.

Complimentary healing methods are not a replacement for medical treatment nor should they ever be referred to as a promised cure. Conventional medical advice should always be sought in the first instance and a therapist should ask for written permission from your doctor prior to commencing any therapy if they have any doubt as to whether you are able to receive a treatment.

Trauma in our lives often causes us to look more at our spiritual needs and that's where holistic therapies can be of great comfort and help with regard to healing. Most therapies can be beneficial as they all tap into the same immaculate universal energy within and around us. It's just a matter of personal choice which one suits you as an individual.

Spiritual Healing

Spiritual healing (incidentally, not based as many people believe on any religious practice) is a non-invasive, simple, gentle method of healing, which can have a profoundly positive effect on emotional, physical and spiritual balance. In turn it promotes better health and understanding of our origins. (The National Federation of Spiritual Healers is listed in the contacts section at the back of this book).

After I had received spiritual healing some years ago, I was astonished with the wonderful results. It enabled me to find inner reserves of strength I never knew existed and within a month of receiving healing I was able to change my career direction, face my fear of flying and became a cabin crew member with the 'world's favourite airline!'.

Reiki Healing

Reiki healing (Rei - means 'Universal' and Ki - means 'energy' in Japanese) is a non-invasive natural therapy based on ancient methods of healing practice that offers balance of the body, mind, emotional and spiritual healing of any *living* being. Reiki healing is a relaxing and powerful healing method that channels Universal life force energies which we all have within and around us and that we all have natural access to. It can be used on anyone or anything!

Both spiritual and Reiki healing sessions usually last between 30 minutes and an hour and include the lightest of non-invasive touch and occasional gentle communication from the healer (possibly more so with spiritual healing) to encourage you to relax and release any tensions you may have. The stimulation that healing provides in any form of therapy can have a profound effect on the body as a whole and encourages the mind, body and spirit to be in balance.

The power of these remarkable forms of healing has been used to bring about relief from many illnesses and stress and a sense of peace and acceptance in terminally ill patients for centuries before us.

Always contact a professional healer and search for one who suits you. The session should be a purely pleasurable and nurturing experience. Both spiritual and Reiki healing are 100% safe and can be used on babies, children, the elderly, pets and even plants. Neither forms of healing are linked to a religion and they have no connections with cults or special belief systems. They don't involve hypnosis or massage and are not just for when you are ill. Healing is for everyone, not just a limited few! There's no need to disrobe for either as both these forms of healing take effect through clothing. Belief in these methods of healing is not a requirement, only a willingness to relax, be open and a desire to be healed.

Pure Essential Oils

The 19th and 20th Centuries witnessed the creation of the many synthetic drugs and chemicals that are in use today and this took over from the use of natural herbal medicine and remedies at great speed.

Thanks to the French chemist Rene Gate Fosse in 1937, 'aromatherapy' was born. One day whilst in his laboratory he accidentally burnt his hand and plunged it into the nearest bowl of liquid he could find. It happened to contain essential oil of lavender and to his amazement his hand healed extremely quickly and with very little scarring. With further research and experimentation, aromatherapy then took off around the world to form one of the strongest forms of complimentary medicine in use today.

Great care should be taken when using essential oils. Always read the instructions carefully before using natural oils as they can have powerful and immediate effects. There are certain oils which should not be used on babies and children or during the first three months of pregnancy. In these instances, you will need to consult your pharmacists for advice.

To make sure you are getting the *real* thing look for oils that have the words *pure essential oil* written on the bottle. There are fabulous ranges available and those that I have listed below are just some of the most popular and pleasant to use. They can be used as alternatives to room fragrances or mixed with an almond oil base for use in the bath, or for gentle massage, and are perfect 'balancing' oils.

Geranium

Good for balancing the hormones and moods! It's used a lot in massage as it is good for skin conditions and has a stimulating effect on the lymphatic system.

Grapefruit

A great *releasing* oil and good for clarity of mind. Releases pent up or stale feelings.

Jasmine

One of the most expensive oils with a sensual exotic fragrance. It's fabulous for beating stress and is best used in massage. It's also known as a great aphrodisiac!

Lemongrass

A *strengthening* oil, excellent if you are suffering from burn out and/or nervous exhaustion.

Lavender

Probably the best-known essential oil. Lavender helps to stimulate the immune system and has many other benefits. This wonderful essence is perfect for many psychological and physical conditions having calming and antiseptic qualities. Dab a few drops on a tissue and have near by to soothe and nurture.

Neroli

Otherwise known as orange blossom oil, Neroli is a great stress reliever and smells beautiful!

Oil of Orange

Has a great uplifting fragrance and is good if you suffer from lack of energy or depression.

Patchouli

Helps to ease apprehension and bring about clarity of mind.

Rose

Although this can be a little expensive, natural rose oil is lovely for sensuality and relaxation.

Rosemary

Lovely for bathing or massage and is a good psychological stimulant. Helps to give clarity of thought, lifts lethargy and poor memory yet calms the mind and body beautifully. Also great to use when studying.

Ylang Ylang

Instils confidence and has a warming fragrance. It can help with emotions such as anger, fear of failure, impatience, panic attacks and lack of self-esteem.

It is also known to be an effective and sensuous aphrodisiac.

On the subject of lovely smells, incense sticks have been used for centuries to clear negative energies, not to mention gets rid of nasty smells too! Some are used for health purposes, particularly those made by the Tibetan monks. Thankfully they are now easy to obtain through good spiritual shops.

Most of all, investigate, explore and enjoy everything good in life!

Reflexology

Reflexology is a remarkable natural non-invasive therapy where the therapist stimulates more than 7,000 nerves whilst touching the feet. This in turn encourages the opening and clearing of neural pathways, immediately improves the blood and lymphatic circulation and can help relieve many conditions. The hands also contain thousands of nerves and, as with the feet, replicate each corresponding side of the body in miniature. Although the majority of therapists work on the feet, some therapists, including myself, perform reflexology on the hands as well, with the same wonderful healing effects.

Every part of the body functions with the help of messages carried back and forth along the neural pathways. These pathways consist of living tissue and electrical channels and can become impaired by many factors. When they become impaired, nerve function is impeded. Messages are delivered slowly and unreliably, or not at all, and the body processes operate at less than optimum levels.

Since ancient times healers have employed various methodologies to strengthen and balance the energy flow in our bodies. Many therapies including acupuncture, shiatsu and reflexology agree that this energy flows in zones or meridians throughout the body. Reflexologists specify that there are ten energy zones that run the length of the body from head to toe, five on each side of the body ending in each foot and running down arms into the tips of the fingers. By applying light pressure to a specific zone, the entire zone it relates to in the body is stimulated. For instance, by stimulating a zone on the foot which corresponds with the kidneys, you can help to release vital energy that may be blocked somewhere within that zone. By working on the kidney reflex area on the foot, it revitalizes and balances the entire zone in this area of the body as well as helping to improve the function of the organ itself.

Reflexology *stimulates* the bodies 'neural' pathways known as energy zones, unblocking, stimulating, detoxifying and re-balancing the body to a natural state. Energy circulates unconsciously throughout the body on a physical, emotional and mental level. There is also energy of the spirit that is just as crucial to our over-all well-being as our physical or mental energy.

By stimulating what in the East is known as 'Chi' (energy) along your neural pathways it enhances healing energy to flow smoothly, balancing the body as a whole. The sleep and relaxation, which is induced by reflexology treatments, is pure instant healing.

Scientifically, all forms of energy need to be revitalized periodically. According to the polarity theory, it must flow unimpeded between the negative and positive poles that every atom and cell contains and in oriental thought the 'Yin' and 'Yang' energy currents must compliment each other to bring about and maintain a natural state of balance.

Reflexology, as with most other natural therapies, reduces stress by generating deep and tranquil relaxation. Lying down is the first step to relaxation. Sensory nerve endings send information to the spinal cord and brain, which in turn send information to the organs and muscles.

The lymphatic system (part of our immune system) runs alongside our blood circulation and is a crucial dumping ground for dead blood cells and viruses. Lymphatic drainage is something that can be performed as an individual therapy in itself. During reflexology treatments, by applying specific stimulation to the lymphatic reflex areas found in the feet or hands, natural lymphatic drainage can be encouraged.

- To pamper yourself with a reflexology home treatment try to pay more attention to both your hands and feet when bathing. Massage and apply cream to them after your bath to maximise the healing powers of touch. The inside edge of each foot represents each side of your spine. Gently run your thumb down these edges. Massaging your feet and hands regularly can have a remarkable effect on helping you to feel more relaxed.

- Stimulate your soles! Go bare foot whenever and wherever you can for as long as you can. We are naturally and gently stimulated by the power of touch and contact with the ground through the thousands of nerve receptors in our feet.

- A lovely reflexology massage to do for yourself to both stimulate your circulation and to relax you is to do what is known as 'foot fanning' on the soles of your feet. After bathing apply a little cooling foot lotion to your feet and, gently supporting your foot with your fingers around the sides, slide your thumbs over your feet starting from just beneath your toes. Cross both thumbs over each other down the soles in a 'crossing' action widthways. Do the same on the top of your foot and finish by gently massaging the feet towards the direction of your heart.

- A lovely way to relax is to massage some natural body cream into your sensuous ankles.

This wonderfully sensitive area represents the reproductive and lymphatic systems.

A fantastic way to give yourself a natural therapy is to give yourself a back and foot scrub. It stimulates the circulation, thus, your energy, at cellular level.

*　*　*

Awareness of the Chakras – Our Natural Energy Fields

There are seven major energy centre areas within the auric field in our bodies called Chakras (from the Sanskrit word meaning Wheel of Fire). It's important for us to be aware that they are all constantly moving and that a free-flow of these energies has a direct impact on our health and well-being. From the crown of our heads to the base of our spine they merge with each other at intervals and correspond with the endocrine glands in our body, each having a vital function to transmit chemical hormones around our body. The glands and consequently, the chakras, work to attract positive energy vibration. Areas of imbalance can lead to physical, mental or emotional imbalance, which are easily detected at times of illness.

The method of dowsing, using natural crystal pendulums can help to detect energy imbalance with astonishing accuracy! I have successfully used this method as a therapist prior to treatments to detect any imbalance which my clients may or may not be aware of. This guidance enables me to work towards re-balancing the body as a whole. It's rather like having a satellite navigation detection system prior to treatments!

Animals also have chakra areas very similar to the positioning of our human energy centres and imbalance can just as easily be detected. I have had some very accurate and wonderful results from treating both humans and animals with the combination of crystal pendulum readings and Reiki healing.

Working with and understanding our vital chakra areas play a large part of awareness in the practice of yoga and has done for thousands of years before us.

The '**crown chakra**' on the top of your head has the function of thought and is portrayed in **purple** or magenta colours. It represents the brain and pineal gland, which is important for the release of the hormones, which help regulate our biological clock. This area is also linked to inner strength and spirituality and is associated with all the other charkas. If the area of the crown chakra shows an imbalance it could indicate that other areas may need balancing.

The '**brow chakra**', also known as the 'third eye chakra', is located between your eyes. It is represented by the colour **violet** and is associated with the area of the third eye and is said to correspond with your pituitary gland, which governs the hormones of other endocrine glands and is linked to all physical functions.

The **'throat chakra'** represents your creativity and expression of voice. It is blue in colour and represents the area of the thyroid gland and the throat area, giving freedom of speech and creative expression.

The **'heart chakra'** represents love and is represented as **green** in colour and is associated with your cardiac energies.

The **'solar plexus chakra'** (found just above your naval) represents wisdom and energy and is represented by the colour **yellow**. This is known as the nerve centre area of your body, representing total emotional and physical balance.

The **'sacral chakra'** represents your vitality, incorporating joy and abundance in your life. Found mid way between the solar plexus and the root chakra, it is **orange** in colour and represents your adrenal glands, which regulate adrenaline balances and the spleen.

The **'base chakra'** or 'root chakra' can be found at the base of the spine. It represents physicality and is **red** in colour, which is the main grounding colour. It represents the base of your life-force energy and your reproductive area.

The main chakra I want to tell you about and raise awareness of when recovering from M.E./C.F.S. anxiety, depression and coping with stress, is the **'solar plexus chakra'**, which is the largest and most powerful of the

Elizabeth Bailey

chakras and represents the **autonomic nervous system** which regulates all natural involuntary responses within your body. It's also linked to the **pancreas** and **liver,** which look after the purifying process of the digestive system and the balance of insulin, and control the sugar levels in your bloodstream.

On an emotional level the colour yellow represents confidence. A healthy balance in this area shows that you radiate self-control and have good general balance. The solar plexus area in your body is the area just under your chest in the centre, where your ribs meet internally and is about a hand's width above your naval. 'Solar' relates to the 'Sun' and 'plexus' means 'main area'.

It's in the area of the Solar Plexus that all nerves meet up and it's also believed to be our main spiritual centering point - *the main energy area of our beings*, and factually it's also the last area in our bodies to die.

Readings of energy balances can be taken by dowsing, holding a crystal pendulum over the body, concentrating on the chakra areas to define if there's an imbalance anywhere. The crystal is held over each of the charka areas starting from the crown while the recipient is lying down. If the pendulum swings erratically or the movement is weak this is understood to mean that there is an energy imbalance in that particular area.

When holding a pendulum over a chakra area, if it rotates in circles or in a petal shape of a flower, the energy levels in that area are good. In fact the strength of movement and timing of swing indicates the strength of the energy flow. The rest of the body's chakra areas are then covered in line. When the readings are complete, the pendulum is then moved back to any weaker areas and the reading is taken again.

Areas of imbalance can be helped to be re-balanced either through the positive energy of the crystal pendulum, healing, or meditation, and through asanas in yoga or even sound therapy through humming. It's important to be aware of these particular areas because the body is linked as a whole entity, dowsing and being *aware* of this helps to restore balanced energy levels.

- Here's an excellent tip for calming and to see which way your energy wheel turns! Give your solar plexus area a gentle clockwise rub in circles with your hand and see how it feels. Do it slowly, ten times clockwise then observe how it feels. Then try doing it in an anti-clockwise direction, again ten times, and compare which way felt best. You can help to calm and soothe yourself by doing this in 'your way' at anytime.

The Healing Power of the Earth's Crystals

Everything in our physical world has an energy vibration, a sound, a light, you and me!

Over 10,000 million years ago, our Universe was created with an astronomical explosion. The gas from this outbreak formed galaxies and stars. During the next 5,000 million years planet Earth was created from the immense cloud of gas and dust particles in the atmosphere.

The Earth consists of three layers: the crust, the mantle and the core. The crust is where crystals and gemstones are found.

For thousands of years crystals and gemstones have been used in rituals and were used as offerings to the Gods, charms of protection and aids to healing. Crystals are frequently mentioned in the Bible and are considered as sacred in many parts of the World. To the Native American and Mexican race the crystal **Turquoise** is still to this day considered to be sacred and there's evidence that the Egyptians have used the healing power of crystals for centuries. The spellbinding powers, beauty and mysticism of natural crystals are now thankfully being rediscovered all over the world to help with the healing of our emotional, physical and spiritual equilibrium.

Each crystal or rock formation is said to have its own special balancing effects. From calming **amethyst, rose quartz, blue lace agate** and **quartz crystal** to uplifting **citrine,** they all have particular healing properties and can have a remarkable effect on our emotions There's an enormous variety available and if you can find a good supplier it's wonderful to build up a beautiful collection to help balance your moods and assist your healing process.

A mere thought held in your mind, that crystals may help to heal you is a good thing and truly healing in itself.

Whether you believe in the healing power of crystals or not, they are beautiful objects created from nature by the powers of our Universe. They are used in many holistic therapies to calm and balance the body and mind with remarkable results.

If the power of suggestion in your mind is a 'good' one then be it a crystal, a positive thought, or a good wish then it's still part of helping yourself to heal.

Crystals can be used to heal the chakras. Choose colours that relate to the colour of each chakra and place directly above the chakra to bring about balance.

The one that had an effect for me personally was **heamatite** which is reputed to be a grounding crystal. Many years ago I bought a bracelet made of haematite and wore it until one day it broke. With my haematite beads flying all over my workplace floor, I scrambled to retrieve them, but didn't get around to threading them up again. Some years later I was told by a spiritual healer that was a sign that I no longer needed to be grounded! However, there came a time when I did feel the need to be grounded once more and I threaded my haematite bracelet together again. I tied numerous knots in the elastic and began to wear it again. I was so pleased I'd found it, because it's also nice to look at. Then, just as before, it broke again and burst all over the floor! Once again I gathered up every bead for the next time that I needed grounding! Since then, I've studied these beautiful crystal formations further and have found that they have been of great help in my work as a therapist and healer.

Quartz crystal is a natural oscillator. It receives, transforms and stores energy and is used in watches and machinery for precision and accuracy.

These beautiful creations of the Universe come from the beginning of time. Given as a gift to someone to help him or her heal is a beautiful personal gesture and buying one for yourself is even more powerful!

Choosing Crystals

It's believed that you should choose crystals that you feel 'drawn to' because your mind, body and spirit instinctively know what you need at any one time and you'll make a natural choice based on that feeling.

There are some excellent books on crystals available. I discovered that some opinions about them and their specific powers differ slightly so I suggest it's worth buying whichever book you are drawn to. I used them to help our situation with M.E./C.F.S. and like with many of the topics covered in this book, I took a closer look at many things in life in general when my Son and I became unwell and discovered some wonderful finds! I always have, and probably always will, be drawn to possess crystals. I suggest you have a look and see if you're drawn to any yourself. Ideally, seek out a place with a good selection of crystals that supplies books about them. I usually find that if that's the case, it's a good sign that you should also be able to get advice on how to care for the crystal of your choice.

Just like us, crystals can pick up negative energies - being natural it's only to be expected! Here are a few ways to cleanse them:

- Run them under cold water for 1 minute and dry in direct sunlight, or on a south-facing windowsill or in the light of a full moon (try to minimise the time that coloured crystals are left in direct sunlight to avoid fading).

- Energise them by washing them in a clear stream or even better the sea. What a fantastic way to relax, roll the trousers up and paddle! The energies of the sea are so potent. (Seawater itself is reputed to be healing).

- You can blow away the negative energies (literally).

- Other ways include burying them in your garden to be re-energised by the soil of the Earth and its unique energy; you just have to remember where you buried them!

- Putting them into sea salt in a large jar overnight.

- Literally just rest your crystals onto a bed of amethyst crystal as it has self-cleansing properties.

As mentioned earlier, crystal tea light holders are perfect for bedrooms. With care they are safe to leave flickering while you relax, giving off their healing glow.

Rose quartz is a perfect crystal for the bedroom as it's said to encourage self-love, love of others around us and helps to restore emotional balance. A nice way to keep your body in contact with crystals is to keep a tumble stone size crystal with you in a pocket. Another great way to benefit from their energy is to hold or place them near to you when doing your relaxation/meditation.

*It's believed that if you carry a piece of **Citrine** in your purse it's said that the purse will never be empty... You could try them and see but most of all ~ enjoy!*

Colour for Healing and Balance

The spectacular rainbow Universal spectrum light colours in natural light bring life and healing to every plant and living cell.

Our natural world is full of colour. 'Colour therapy' is now recognised and used in healing with wonderful results. Colour therapists work by using colour in visualisations and occasionally, with the suggestions of breathing specific colours in and out. By using light treatments colour therapy can achieve fantastic results by using calming colours to help to reduce stress and induce relaxation or, alternatively, using vibrant colours to stimulate energy levels and treat illness.

Colour therapy is also used in medicine, instead of given a blood transfusion, babies born with jaundice are now simply placed under blue light for a period of time...and it works miraculously.

The colours we wear and surround ourselves with is a recognised natural therapy, try experimenting with new colours with your clothes and in your home. Even a change of wall colour can be uplifting, you'll know what suits you best because you'll *feel* it's doing you good!

Wearing different colours can represent how we are feeling and in turn can directly affect our moods. For example, red is a wonderful grounding colour, whereas blue is calming. I suggest you go for whatever colour suits you best, but try to avoid too much black. If you like to wear black however, it can be livened up beautifully by wearing a colourful scarf or tie, and jewellery accessories can look even more stunning when worn with black.

It's a fact that wearing colours to match and enhance your chakra areas is also healing in itself (please see information on chakras in the previous section).

A fantastic way to help bring about balance is to be at one with nature's colours. Calming greens and browns of the forests and the blue of the sea bring calmness. Watch the glowing red, orange and yellow flames of a natural fire to bring comfort and grounding.

Coloured silk on bare skin is a lovely way of bathing yourself in colour, as a therapy. Silk as a natural product in itself against the skin is a beautiful feeling. Silk scarves can be used to lie on your body during relaxation and meditation or sumptuously drape your naked body in as much silk as you can afford!

The suggested self help recommendation is to then lie in direct sunlight covered with the silk in the particular colour you need at the time ~ *bliss.* It also gives the neighbours something to think about!

It's important to never let go of the child within us and keep our world full of colours. Even at the office add a splash of colour with a smart coloured broach or tie pin and silk handkerchief for the chaps and bring in a posy of fresh flowers for your desk. The fragrance of fresh flowers stimulates our senses and our hormones too.

As well as using chakra colours to treat energy areas, colours can be used to treat or stimulate in the following ways:

(Colours marked * are often used in colour therapy)

BLACK

A colour which represents the protection of yourself and having a smart, business like, approach. It can be beneficial in those situations, but may demonstrate a sense that you are hiding behind the colour. It could be taken to mean that you may be unapproachable and want to fade into the background, which is fine if you want to do that! It's not a colour for enlightenment.

*BLUE

The cool colour of blue is used to relax and relieve where there is inflammation. It can be beneficial for helping to lower blood pressure and helps aid restful sleep. On a spiritual level blue is thought to represent communication.

* DARK BLUE

Is also used to help heal the skeletal system with fractures or breaks. Dark shades of blue are contra indicated (not recommended) and therefore should be avoided if suffering from depression.

*GREEN

A cool colour bringing harmony and peace. It calms nerves yet is gently stimulating and is greatly used as a tonic in colour therapy. It particularly helps to ease digestive inflammation and can help the liver if overworked.

* TURQOUISE

Is a variant of green and is helpful if suffering from long periods of stress with calming results and it is often used to uplift and heal emotions.

*INDIGO

Cool and relaxing and used to reduce inflammation, pain or swelling and an overactive sex-drive. Not recommended if suffering from depression but milder hues of purple are softer and have less of a cold effect generally.

*ORANGE

Is a warm, energizing colour that brings joy. It's used to particularly stimulate the respiratory system and is also said to energise the thyroid gland, which balances the metabolism.

*GOLD

Being a softer version of orange is a fantastic healing colour and is used for healing the body, mind and spirit as a whole.

*RED

Says you're ready for action! It is the colour of grounding, bringing the effects of strength and vibrancy. It increases circulation and is good for nervous exhaustion. It stimulates the adrenal glands and can be used to help with low blood pressure. Lighter shades of **PINK** work in a more subtle way and are therefore a good alternative if red is too vibrant for you. Pink is also associated with nurturing and love.

*VIOLET

A cool, relaxing colour, it balances by sedating the nervous system yet stimulates the pineal gland, 'third eye chakra', which is associated with spiritually and with extra sensory perception (ESP). The pineal gland is believed to be responsible for the balance of sleep patterns and is connected to the release of melatonin (our sleep inducing hormone), so this is a great colour for bedrooms. It's not recommended for lack of energy, as it is very much a relaxing colour, but it's great for anxiety and insomnia. Sweet dreams!

WHITE

Colour of purity giving a very approachable feeling, helps brings about balance and harmony when worn.

*YELLOW

A warm energizing colour and good for stimulating the mind, muscular and lymphatic system, it's stimulating effect should be avoided if you suffer from insomnia or at times of nervous tension. **CREAM,** being the softer hue of yellow, is a good colour used for general balancing.

Music for the Soul

Since ancient times music has been used to bring about change in the human condition. Scientifically proven, listening to music directly affects the Limbic system in our primitive brains, which is responsible for our automatic body functions including our emotions and movement. Music has been used in therapy for many years.

The value of sound and music as a therapeutic technique has been acknowledged in areas of psychological and mental health and occupational therapy. Music seems to bypass the minds analytical and logical filters stimulating the memory and imagination.

The high water content of our body's tissues helps to conduct sound waves like a deep massage at cell level! Listening to music brings about confidence and balance of our physical, emotional, mental and spiritual life.

A great way to lift your mood when you wake up is to turn on your favourite piece of feel-good music. It has an incredibly uplifting effect on the mind. Listening to an upbeat piece of music first thing when you wake causes you to release endorphin chemicals in the brain that stay with you for much of the day. Listening to your favourite music before your wind down time before going to bed can also have great therapeutic effects.

It's important to make sure that you listen to the type of music that makes you feel *good* though!

Music and sound are also used to change the energies of an area; the sound of a bell has been used for centuries to ring in changes around the world.

Wind chimes bring subtle changes to an area and specific tones of chimes are said to bring about different changes to inspire, relax or energise according to their tone.

- A great Feng Shui tip to clear out old energies and welcome in the new is to play loud music for ten minutes once a week. After all, no one should complain about ten minutes a week of a little volume at a reasonable time of the day to celebrate life! However, you don't need to play music loud to appreciate its value. Listening to music is one of the best self-help therapies you can treat yourself to.

The Healing Power of the Voice

Singing has been scientifically proven to boost the immune system. Scientific studies of singers showed raised measurements of immunoglobulin E (IgE) in their blood after singing rehearsals proving a powerful link to health and the immune system. It also increases the heart rate, raises energy levels, reduces tension, raises self-esteem and is a fantastic confidence booster.

You don't have to be a perfect singer ~ humming is a fantastic way to clear negative energies at cellular level. For thousands of years chanting and mantras have been practiced worldwide to balance energy levels by both helping to raise energy, and bringing control to the mind.

In yoga practice chakra balancing with sound is represented by producing resonant sounds, which work on the different chakra areas of the body. They are repeated whilst in meditation to re-energise and restore health to the mind, body and spirit.

This can be done easily by sitting with your spine straight, closing your eyes and working through these areas with the following sounds repeating each one in turn three times. Afterwards, sit for a moment or two and check how you feel:

(Sounds are pronounced slightly elongated e.g. Lam = Laam etc.)

Base chakra (lower body level and base of spine) -
    Lam
Sacral chakra (naval height and surrounding area) -
    Wam
Solar Plexus (between lower rib area) - Ram
Heart   (and surrounding area) - Yam
Throat - Ham
3rd Eye (between eyebrows/brain/pineal gland) - Aum

* * *

Singing is therapeutic and also brings about healing. Scientifically proven, singing helps us release the natural happy hormone serotonin. Different types and styles of music have different effects. For instance, dramatic music with discordant sound can stir aggression, this can be useful in a safe environment if you really want to let off steam! Pain-releasing sounds are effectively used safely in sound therapy, so next time you feel like a moan ~ *go with it!*

Bursting into song can also be a great way to diffuse anger!

Singing lullaby's to children has the same magical effect for adults. The words may change but the intent and purpose of singing softly before sleep has been known to be effective in treating insomnia, particularly as the heartbeat is affected by the rhythm of sound vibration.

It's been recorded that foetuses in the womb respond calmly and their heartbeats regulate, when exposed to classical music such as Vivaldi and Mozart. Whereas, they respond by kicking more and their heartbeats are raised when listening to heavy metal!

Singing groups can be a great way to meet new people, build confidence and improve your health and well-being.

In time as you progress, you may even, like me, find yourself singing around the house unexpectedly which is a fantastic sign that you are healing at a deep level, so look out for that and congratulate yourself when it happens!

* * *

Grounding — A Healing Method to Calm and Re-energize

This is a wonderful visualisation technique that can be practiced at anytime to 'centre' oneself. It's a fantastic method to practice in daily situations when you may feel in need of support. It helps to remind us that we are all creations of the Universe and that we can connect back to our roots as part of nature and look at life from the 'bigger picture', to regain perspective and control at anytime.

- Either whilst standing or sitting place your feet flat (preferably bare) on the ground - *do this as much as you can!*

- With your feet about a few inches apart to balance you, make good contact with the ground by gently rolling your feet from side to side and gently back and forth.

- Place your hand gently on your abdomen area (solar plexus). Close your eyes and take two or three good deep breaths through your nose, feeling the rise and fall of your abdomen. If comfortable, keep your eyes closed.

- Imagine that you have roots from the soles of your feet that go deep into the ground that connects you with the Earth's energies.

- On your next 'in' breath imagine a brilliant golden light showering you from above with positive energy. This energy is travelling right down from the crown of your head, downwards through your body. On your 'out' breath imagine that the light is taking with it any negative energy or tension and returning it to the Earth, through your feet, down into your roots and back into the Earth to be re-charged as cosmic positive energy once again. Repeat this three times.

Then picture yourself being wrapped in a sapphire blue cloak for healing and protection and then being encased in a beautiful golden bubble of light for further protection. Slowly open your eyes and re-focus for a moment on your surroundings, tuning in with the sounds that are around you. Take another calming breath ready to continue with the rest of your day feeling refreshed and grounded.

This can be done immediately in situations as a **mini grounding** by simply imagining being filled with the golden light on your 'in' breath and flushing negativity out on your 'out' breath. With practice this method of grounding can produce superb and instant results!

The Healing Power of Touch and the Senses

Touch causes thousands of sensory nerves to be stimulated which results in wonderful chemical reactions in our bodies that bring about feelings of nurturing and pleasure.

I truly believe that touch is one of nature's magical healing energies that's designed to be given from one to another. I learnt this particularly through my work as a therapist. Many people are starved of human touch and even more so of showing their emotions.

Premature babies respond to being touched and their survival is greatly assisted by human touch.

- Touching, as well as receiving touch, stimulates thousands of nerve receptors, which trigger our brain to release feel good hormones (as if you need me to tell you!).

- Hugs are a common acknowledgement and strongly recommended in healing! If you don't like them, practice, just use your judgement on whom. If you haven't got anyone who's handy and obliging to hug with then give yourself a hug – you deserve it.

- Animals, unless wild or in fear, also respond to touch. Yet there are some humans and animals that don't and they miss out on one of our most healing, pleasurable, stimulating and nurturing of all senses.

- I hope we can learn to connect. It costs nothing to give love. I sure I'm not the only person in the world who has an overwhelming desire to hold the hands of people who are upset or unwell.

- It's our choice to get and stay in touch physically and spiritually with ourselves. With relaxation/ meditation practice and positive problem solving and thoughts, we can.

Give yourself a healing head rub. Head massage can be incredibly relaxing. You can simply give yourself a treat by placing all your fingers and thumbs on your scalp and gently rubbing in tiny circles. Use a similar method to when you wash your hair but with a conscious effort to stimulate the scalp, paying particular attention around your temple area, which you can do gently with one finger on each side. Work from front to back and simply indulge and nurture yourself. It's great to get someone to do it for you, but when you do it yourself you know exactly what feels best.

Pamper yourself and gently massage your body at every opportunity

On a cautionary note, if you have M.E./C.F.S. or fatigue try to avoid having a full body massage until you have recovered. However, if you're suffering from stress, anxiety or depression, in-depth massage can be extremely beneficial and can help to relax you. If you have any health concerns, medical permission from your doctor or specialist should be sought before commencing any form of therapy, which involves stimulation to the body. This is particularly true if you have an infection or in cases of chronic illness, diabetes, heart problems, cancer, or prior to or after surgery (at least three months). If you have a viral infection I would not recommend that you have massage or reflexology until you feel better. You'll have something else even more wonderful to look forward to when you start to feel better.

Self-help reflex tips:

- **For extra relief from headaches** gently rub circles on the print of each of your thumbs with the other a few times.

- **To help stress relief** rub the centre of each of your palms clockwise a few times with the thumb of the other hand.

- It's good for the guys as well as the girls to massage both hands fully back and front with hand cream. Running the fingers of the other hand upwards and towards the heart on the back of the other hand between the metacarpal (finger bones) helps to stimulate the energy zones of your chest area.

Flower Power

A great way to instantly bring a powerful positive change of energy and to bring about wonderful balance into your environment is to brighten it up with fresh flowers. They all have their different properties and immaculate naturally therapeutic scents.

If you have a dark, formal corner balance and lighten the space with some feminine flowers with a 'cottage garden' feel such as freesias, lissianthus, astroemerias, gerberas or sweet williams and grasses.

Informal areas can be softened and smartened by adding elegant roses, lilies, amaryllis or ivies, or strike the balance with combinations of lavender and roses, or tulips and gypsophelia.

Bamboo is a great indoor plant bringing with it the ancient belief that a bamboo plant growing in your home brings harmony and prosperity.

On a summer's evening take a walk in your garden or the park and smell the wonderful scent of the flowers. Observe their immaculate way of calling to the insects and birds with their heavenly scent.

Staying Strong

Embracing the Winds of Change

Healing is about change and a vital factor of healing is our own awareness and readiness to accept the 'need' to change. If we are willing we can receive in return the motivation and desire to feel better.

Our mind, body and spiritual functions when balanced can enable us to face our lives with a new approach. Situations still occur in our lives, it's the way life is for each and every one of us, but through awareness we are able to manage those situations with a different approach.

Taking lots of time out to look after ourselves at every moment is crucial to our health and well-being. This is not to deny any pain in our lives. It enables us to *feel* and acknowledge what's really important. As children we delighted in using our senses of smell, taste, sound and rhythm. We only ever lose these senses if we wish to do so. By taking time out often and taking control again we rekindle our spirit and the *pleasures* of life.

As life moves on we notice that people we know and love grow and change. When we learn to be 'open' and let go of the destructiveness of hoarding, either objects or other people in our lives, we are learning to experience the flow of life with it's changing patterns and prove that we are *alive*. By opening up to new energies, people, and situations, this enables our own lives to flourish and grow.

An important part of healing and recovery is to embrace and welcome changes.

- Change is a GOOD thing and is all part of life's rich tapestry!

- We are all evolving and change in our lives enables us to move *forward.*

- Life is all about changes, waves of energy, all of life has ebbs and flows. Our changing seasons, flowing tides, our own moods all carry a flow with them, to calm once more.

- Our minds can be constantly full of chatter. By taking time out and learning to still our minds, we can change the impact and flow of our life enormously and gain inner strength and wisdom. Pain simply can't last forever; thankfully, it's the law of nature.

It's sometimes necessary to remind ourselves that no matter what's troubling us, thankfully, life goes on. The sun always rises the following day and people move about and around us... and a new chapter begins.

It's healthy and creative to try to do something a bit different each day from your normal routine to alleviate boredom and is a great way to help to keep yourself motivated. Bringing as much variety into your life as possible is also a great way to help beat depression.

- Try changing the type of music you listen to.

- Visit the library and read up on different subjects. The Universe is a mind blowing beautiful subject and it sure puts many things into perspective!

- Hire out a new DVD to watch.

- Buy a magazine that you haven't tried before.

- 'Thinking' of as many different small changes you can make or do and writing them down is also a great therapy.

- Going for breakfast out somewhere one morning or two makes a good start to the day. You could try as many different places as you can for breakfast.

- Change your usual walk areas.

- Trying *different* foods, which you've not tried before, can stimulate your senses and shift your energies.

- Try going to different shops at *different* places.

- Refresh body, mind and soul, fly a kite! There are some great ones available in sizes to suit everyone. It's so much fun and *feeds the soul* no matter what age you are!

Adding variety to your life in as many ways as you can helps to create balance and stability within.

Do as many different things as you can even if they seem a bit odd - it's different, fun and is a great way to disarm depression.

Laugh in the Face of Adversity

It's a fact that a good laugh can help your body to heal and brings about a fantastic feeling of well-being!

Factually, it's estimated that people who laugh for as little as 15 minutes a day are likely to suffer less from heart disease and high blood pressure.

Truly the best medicine, laughter stimulates the Thymus gland releasing natural 'feel good' hormones into our bodies. It helps strengthen our immune system and our blood flow is increased as blood vessels expand when we laugh. Therefore, laughing pretty much has the same effect as cardiovascular exercise but without the strain!

As if that's not good enough, it physically *rocks the heart* and revitalizes our energies and boosts our immune system, as our breathing becomes deeper when we have a good chuckle. *Preferably belly laugh!*

- Top tip: Sit comfortably and tilt your head back and give a hearty laugh ~ if you keep going you'll even laugh naturally at yourself. *Try it and see.*

Learning to laugh and be happy is a skill, which we can all practice. It's remarkable how, once we tune into it we can respond by then laughing and finding the funny side of many situations, *even stressful ones.* Just as we get used to being stressed, our body responds *even better* to the good vibrations of laughter, which improves our health and raises our self-esteem.

FACT: Tears of sadness contain a different chemical compound to tears of laughter and joy.

FACT: Scientific medical studies have proved that 'happy people' live longer.

Giving your mind a break by treating yourself to heavy portions of humour works wonderfully ~ provide yourself with fun and laugh your way to future happiness!

Positive Reasons for Smiling

- Smiling uses all of the muscles in our face therefore you're toning your face every time you smile.

- Smiling also brings about feelings of well-being.

- Smiling is contagious! And is medicinal to you and others around you as long as it comes from a place of love – YOU!

- Forget wrinkles. It's far better to be happier on the inside instead of fearing that you're face might crack.

- If someone's lost their smile – give them one of yours.

- Smile and laugh as much as humanly possible even if you don't feel like it. Do the old 'looking into a mirror trick' and smile every time at yourself and often.

There's nothing more positive than sharing a smile with someone.

Fresh Air and Sunshine

It's been proven that people who spend much of their time outside living under canvas have less health problems.

Try to air all of your rooms daily even in winter. Double glazing, central heating and air conditioning can dry the air dramatically and can also increase the harbouring of microscopic mould spores, and viruses love our heating systems! Open windows even just for five minutes a day and, if possible, it's nice to try to keep a small window open in your bedroom overnight for a gentle flow of air.

Stand at an open window, or even better still, get out in the air every day. Breathing in fresh air helps to revive you.

Natural light is one of nature's tonics and has a nutritional value causing subtle chemical changes within our body. It helps to encourage the body's natural healing process and to prevent illness and disease.

Try and be in natural light as much as you can. Sit near a window in your office or take a holiday in a sunny climate in the winter. As far as light goes nothing beats full spectrum natural light.

Avoid fluorescent lights as much as possible. Their inventor never intended them to be used in such vast quantities and as they continuously flicker they can cause headaches, irritability and fatigue. Natural spectrum light bulbs are a great alternative and their arrival has seen much of the departure of the modern condition of Seasonal Affective Disorder Syndrome

(SADS) and many other modern conditions, which is fantastic news!

I also recommend exposing your whole body to sunlight whenever possible, (with obvious care taken not to burn or over expose!). Our skin absorbs vitamin D from natural sunlight and sun 'bathing', literally should be just that.

Getting out daily in just twenty minutes of daylight, summer or winter, helps our bodies to heal.

Sunlight helps to improve our mood, bone strength, energy levels, boost our immune systems and it's even rumoured to enhance fertility.

Be Surrounded by Beauty in Every Season

- Try to visit the ocean and smell the air, walk on the beach barefoot in summer and feel the sand between your toes. Allow yourself to be soothed by the sound of the sea, or hear the crunching of the pebbles beneath your feet. In winter observe the energy in the crashing waves. As the waves roll in feel, hear and breathe in their positive vibrant energy. As you breathe out and the waves subside and return, imagine any tiredness and negativity flowing back out to sea so it can be charged positively once more.

- Wind, sun, rain and snow, savour the changing seasons, particularly our abundance of breathtaking landscapes, villages and countryside. Discover and observe the changing landscapes of our counties as their beauty unfolds before you.

- Crisp Autumn air, Autumn sunlight through the trees in the forest, the smell of the woods in November, remind us that the Earth is preparing for Winter then, once again Spring. Reminding us that thankfully *the wheel of life is forever changing and renewing.*

Try to keep warm. The body uses up enormous amounts of energy when trying to keep warm, particularly when tired. Don't get cold - wear thin layers and strip off if necessary!

Every moment counts. If the moment has passed,
A brand new moment has begun.

Muscle Care

To combat aching muscles through **overwork** take warm baths. Make sure your body is covered with the water as much as possible for maximum effect and massage yourself gently always working towards the heart.

Our muscles, if strained, need to be replenished with blood supply.

For pulled muscles in the neck and shoulders (this may sound a bit brutal and be prepared for a bit of discomfort):

- Sink the tips of your fingers quite firmly into the aching muscle of your opposite arm. From the shoulder inward press and release along the length of the muscle affected. Do this four or five times in succession. Then smooth out with the flat of your hand and rest.

If you have strained muscles through **injury** keep the area cool by applying a cool compress to reduce inflammation and always seek medical advice if the condition persists.

* * *

Tips to Help Calm and Cleanse

This is a great Shiatsu self-help method to **combat restless sleep and insomnia:**

- Preferably sit comfortably on the floor and bring one knee up and place your corresponding elbow for support on your knee. Then place your thumb flat onto the area between your eyebrows on the bridge of your nose and lean onto the thumb holding the pressure for about 10-15 seconds, release and repeat.

Another, is to **clear your sinuses**, which is great for facial circulation too:

1. Support one hand (elbow bent) on a table.

2. Place your thumb and third finger on the area at the beginning of your eyebrow, at the side of the bridge of your nose each side.

3. Then with your index finger press the 'third eye' chakra area at the bridge of your nose.

4. Press your thumb and third finger up into your sinus area, at the same time press inward on the bridge of your nose for about 10 seconds and release.

You see people doing this sometimes naturally if they have a headache. This helps to stimulate the sinuses bringing fresh blood supply into the area. The area should feel refreshed and relaxed afterwards.

Feel the energies between you and a partner!

- Interestingly, a great little trick you could try with a partner or very close friend, is to feel each other's energy levels through your 'third eye' chakras. If you are both sensitive you can get a fantastic buzz from each other. Simply try and get your brows (third eye chakra areas) as close as possible without touching and you should both get a cosmic fuzzy feeling going on. It's fairly addictive!

Take a Mini-Holiday

Don't ever lose that lovely smile of yours. Take yourself on a mini holiday in your mind to refresh your outlook and your mind.

Once you are relaxed and in a state of quiet meditation, be aware of any noises there are outside or within your room. Start to scan your body, beginning at your toes. Relax every section of your body in turn and when you have reached your head area, take yourself on an imaginary journey back to a place in your life where you were really happy and relaxed. Try to focus on the thought that it's just 'you' there. Happy to be just YOU. Maybe you are on holiday or you remember sitting in the sunshine in a beautiful place. If you can't think of an occasion, make one up and add all the trimmings! For instance, imagine you are sitting or laying in the warm sunshine on a smooth rock and hearing the sea in the background gently lapping onto the seashore. Imagine as you breathe, clean and pure fresh air entering your lungs and feel the sense of peace and freedom within you as your whole body melts with relaxation.

Savour the feelings for as long as you want to and 'be there' in your mind. When you feel ready, gently bring yourself back. Slowly imagine coming away from your beautiful place as the sun slowly begins to set behind you, knowing that you can always return, at anytime. Gradually bring yourself back to your surroundings, hearing any noises that are around you and when you open your eyes you should be feeling refreshed and relaxed. Slowly come up to a sitting position and enjoy the rest of your day with a new, happy and relaxed mind.

Happiness is…
THE IMPORTANCE OF ENJOYING EVERY MOMENT

Bring your Awareness to your Breath

A relaxing, yet, energy releasing yogic breath exercise to bring about balance is the BEE BREATH, which is so beneficial to know. It's so simple, yet extremely powerful. It works on a vibratory level by stimulating the brain. The powerful vibration of sound works at cellular level with fantastically calming, yet energising results.

- Make sure you won't be disturbed in any way and sit with your back straight (legs crossed if comfortable) and close your eyes.

- Place both hands over your ears fairly firmly and take a good slow deep breath in through your nose then on the exhalation release the breath slowly again through your nose making a humming sound through your nostrils.

- The sound should be fairly loud and powerful inside your head and you may find that the tune vibration feels quite different from inside your head. Adjust the sound to what feels comfortable for you and repeat five times. Observe how you are feeling for a moment before slowly opening your eyes.

* * *

Catch your energies with your fingertips!

A lovely way to calm yourself down in times of stress or when winding down for sleep, is to capture your natural energies with your fingertips. The yogis have been doing it for centuries by using a very similar method to practice their wonderful mantras. Special cameras can record the sight of the immaculate energies, which emanate from the body and form the aura. The area surrounding the hands is particularly strong.

A simplified version of this exercise is to simply sit with your back straight and comfortable, close your eyes and relax your hands onto your knees (palms facing upward). Your fingers and thumbs should naturally curl inwards. Enhance this by taking deep slow breaths through your nose without force and touch each of your fingertips in turn, with your thumbs starting with your index finger and working through to your small fingers then work back through to your index fingers to finish. Before opening your eyes be *aware* of how you are feeling.

The Calming Breath

Practice of 'THE CALMING BREATH' as well as calming and re-oxygenating your body, can be fantastic for disarming hurried thoughts too.

215

Elizabeth Bailey

It's important to our health and well-being to learn to re-oxygenate our bodies and be aware that shallow breathing can leave stale air in our lungs. Deeper breathing promotes health and vitality, it can also help us to have higher resistance to infections and can help to increase our energy levels and is especially good after any time of immobility or after sleep.

To take better care of your breathing a fantastic yoga breathing technique used to cleanse and re-energise is the 'calming breath'.

As our lungs are all different sizes, regulate timing to suit your size. This exercise must be done gently and slowly without force of any kind and can be practiced *anywhere*.

- Preferably lie or sit down and place one hand gently resting on your chest and the other on your solar plexus area/diaphragm.

- Gently close your eyes and take a slow breath in through your nostrils feeling your diaphragm rise and your ribs expand out to each side. Pause for a second and release the air from your lungs on a slow 'out' breath, emptying your lungs a little more, only for about two seconds more than the 'in' breath.

- Repeat this inhalation and exhalation nine times, concentrating on being aware of your diaphragm and breathing deep into your lungs.

Then return your breathing to its normal pattern, feeling refreshed and relaxed and ready to continue with the rest of your day.

Releasing Tension

A great and natural response to stress is to give a big sigh. Raise your shoulders as you take a deep breath in, then hold it for a second and as you release your breath, lower your shoulders and give a great big sigh like never before, really go for it! Try doing three in succession and see how good it feels!

Summary

During your recovery you may feel that you aren't progressing as fast as you would like, but persevere and don't give up. You'll then find when you do start to pick up that you'll feel even better. It's good to remind ourselves after commencing a period of healing just how far we've progressed on our journey from the start, whether it's physically, mentally, emotionally or spiritually.

Try not to worry if you come across a few set backs in your recovery, it's all part of life and therefore, to be expected, but each step you take *forward* will lead you on and by carefully working through the grey areas you'll be taking steps in leaps and bounds to recovery in the long run.

Watch out for yawns! Of course I'm not suggesting that you just give up at the first sign of one. It sounds simple, but a yawn is the way our autonomic nervous systems (the system that we don't consciously control) tells us that we are 'tired'. It triggers nerve impulses so that our lungs draw in more oxygen to satisfy our bodies needs, but how often do we *really* take notice of our yawns? Simply raising your feet slightly, on a pillow above head level, if it feels comfortable, is an excellent way of refreshing yourself in an instant.

There is the subject of competition. It's a personal matter in any aspect of life and it's far more pleasurable to have a healthy regard for competitiveness and not to be consumed by it. However, *life is not a competition* and it's important that we view our recovery that way.

Tips to take note of:

- Try to sleep if you are tired, sit if you're standing and don't just sit when you can lie down.
- Just like boy scouts, "be prepared". Taking a couple of minutes to prepare things in advance cuts down energy consumption and stress, if you are going out the next day or when you take a holiday. It's far less stressful to start gathering items together in advance. Holiday clothes and toiletries can be stored in an area ready to pack the night before you leave and a day bag can be placed by the front door, so that all you need to do is grab it on your way out.
- 'Listen' to your body and respond, it will pay you dividends in return!

Our energy in life *is* sacred and it's as human beings with a *healthy* natural desire to survive that makes us even more determined to reach for the stars.

Each step you take forward is one less to be taken back.

You Time

When was the last time you did something purely for you and spoilt yourself?

To have a 'me' day is pure self-love and healing!

Spoil yourself even further:

- Take a long soak in a bath surrounded by tea light candles.

- Cook yourself an extra special meal with candles and fresh flowers or even better get someone to do it for you.

- Buy or pick yourself a bunch of flowers. It doesn't need to be extravagant, a single rose to show all-important *self love* is ideal.

- Have a manicure or a pedicure, facial or new hairstyle.

- Do a little bit of retail therapy with a friend for an hour. Just window-shopping helps to beat boredom.

- Girls! Buy a new pot of nail varnish or a new lipstick, it's good girlie fun and you never know your luck!

- Put on your favourite dance music and have a ball! The movement of dance is so therapeutic!

- Why not call The British Wheel of Yoga? (Their telephone number is at the back of this book). They will be able to give you details of professionally trained teachers in your area and you can look forward to a lifetime of learning to balance the mind, body and spirit. (Some of the teachers also have programmes specifically for people who suffer from M.E./C.F.S., so they are ideal). The practice of yoga can also be perfect when it comes to dealing with anxiety, depression and stress related conditions.

- Maybe you could investigate the Doctor/Healer Network: (Please see the contact section).

The Doctor Healer Network greatly acknowledges the practice of healing as being a natural powerful phenomenon, which can be helpful in a whole range of physical and psychological illnesses. The network exists to promote the use of healing in modern clinical practice, independent of any other particular philosophy or tradition.

Doctors who are interested in healing or practice healing or refer patients to healers are involved in the network. By contacting the Doctor Healer network you can be given details of doctors who support healing practice or be directed to healers who work along side doctors and nurses in your area.

The contacts section at the back of this book also contains a number of other organisations and support centres that can provide information. They have also given their much-appreciated support to this book and its purpose.

Golden Suggestions

Live each and every day and every moment to the full.

Breathe some *fresh* air each day.

Feel everything you can touch, especially in nature.

Sense every emotion and accept that life is all about balance.

Be aware and observe yourself learning and growing through your mistakes, knowing that setbacks will make you stronger.

Know that when you come across upset, ask yourself what you may have learned through it; there are lessons to be learned from everything we experience.

When you begin to learn what your body, mind and spirit really needs you are recovering at maximum speed.

As you progress, gradually decrease relaxation routines from 3 times a day for about two months to twice daily, then once according to your recovery needs and rate – BUT NEVER STOP RELAXING!

Gradually decrease the duration of each relaxation from 20 minutes down to 15 minutes, as you progress with your recovery.

Gradually increase walk times, pace and distance ~ try to walk every other day.

Sit quietly with your eyes gently closed every day for five minutes each day the rest of your life and simply just 'BE'.

Restrain yourself on high days and stick to your relaxation routine no matter how you're feeling.

Take one whole day a week to do 'nothing'. No exercise, including no walking, simply just rest and potter.

Pace yourself at all times for the rest of your life and recommend it to *everyone* you know!

Take care of yourself in every way; closely watch that your food intake is good for you.

Try to teach yourself the practice of positive thinking and doing. Although it may not feel like it at the time, you have all the answers you need yourself. If you feel that you don't, you can always ask for 'guidance' from others both on the Earth and spiritual planes.

Plan your future and aim for goals. It's healthy to look forward and even healthier to not look back.

As well as regular relaxation and meditation times and *whenever* you get the chance, lie flat on the floor, close your eyes breathe in and think to yourself:

I breathe in light - as you breathe in

I breathe out darkness – as you breathe out

I breathe in harmony

I breathe out conflict

I breathe in energy

I breathe out tiredness

Elizabeth Bailey

I breathe in life

I breathe out tension

Then roll over onto your right side, bring your knees up towards your chest and rest with your eyes closed for a moment. Then gradually when you feel ready, gently open your eyes. Slowly bring yourself up to sit, close your eyes once again momentarily and very gently run your fingers over your eyelids three times from the centre outwards to refresh them.

From Me to You

And last but by no means least I suggest…

Anything is possible

Never give up and never give in

*We have the here and now, that's what matters,
right here, right now*

Live for the moment

Seek and you will find

Useful Contacts

National Federation of Spiritual Healers NFSH (U.K)

(For details of registered healers in your area.) Tel: 0845 123 2777 www.nfsh.org.uk

Doctor Healer Network U.K.
27, Montefiore Court,
Stamford Hill,
London
N16 5TY

Tel: 020 8800 3569

The Triangle Healing Trust
West Sussex (UK)

Tel: 01444 417198

www.trianglehealingtrust.org
info@trianglehealingtrust.org

Florence House (Retreat)
West Sussex (UK)

Tel: 01323 873700
www.florencehouse.co.uk
info@florencehouse.co.uk

The UK Reiki Federation
(For details of qualified Reiki healers in your area)

Tel: 0870 850 2209
www.reikifed.co.uk
enquiry@reikifed.co.uk

<u>International Federation</u> <u>of Reflexologists</u> (For details of registered Reflexologists in your area)	Tel: 0208 645 9134 <u>www.intfedreflexologists.org</u> <u>ifr44@aol.com</u> <u>info@intfedreflexologists.</u> <u>com</u>
<u>The British Wheel of</u> <u>Yoga</u> (For details of qualified instructors in your area)	Tel: 01529 306851 <u>www.bwy.org.uk</u> <u>office@bwy.org.uk</u>
<u>The Doctor Edward Bach</u> <u>Centre</u>	Tel: 01491 834678 <u>ww.bachcentre.com</u> <u>stefan@bachcentre.com</u>
<u>Alcoholics Anonymous</u> <u>UK help line</u>	0845 769 7555 <u>www.alcoholicsanonymous.</u> <u>org.uk</u>
<u>Sacred Spirits (Spiritual</u> <u>Gifts/crystals)</u> West Sussex (UK)	Tel: 01903 884411 <u>www.sacredspirits.co.uk</u> <u>sacredspirit.69@virgin.net</u>

U.K. M.E/C.F.S. Support

ReMEmember (The Chronic Fatigue Society)	01273 831733 www.remembercfs.org.uk me_cfs@hotmail.com
Association of Young People with M.E. (AYME)	08451 232389 www.ayme.org.uk admin@ayme.org.uk
Edinburgh M.E. Self Help Group	08456 252025 www.edmesh.org.uk membership@edmesh.org.uk
Action for M.E.	Tel: 0845 123 2314 www.afme.org.uk admin@afme.org.uk
M.E/C.F.S. Support Big Step (Website and e-mail support)	www.mesupport.bigstep.com louise@mesupport.bigstep.com

Please note that the contact numbers and website addresses listed were correct at time of publication and are for information purposes only.

About the Author

I have studied many areas of holistic therapy including herbal remedies, iridology, aromatherapy, chakra balancing, in-depth meditation and flower essences and have also trained and worked as a reflexologist.

My journey so far has enabled me to help patients in hospitals and give support at a healing centre to those in need. Having experienced trauma myself, I am able to understand and support the feelings and needs of others, particularly when situations seem to be overwhelming. I have seen the magic that's worked when people arrive at a healing centre, just as I originally did, in search of guidance, and they leave smiling. Confirming that in *truth* we are all 'one' and therefore, can do so much to help one another.

Since going on to write this book I have become a Reiki practitioner. My work has also lead me to other areas and I am at present delighted to be involved in some exiting projects working with children, both in specialist and independent schools and I have met some wonderful people.

I have learnt so much and I am still learning everyday of new and beautiful experiences that only a few years ago I would never have dreamed could happen. I will continue to follow wherever I am 'guided' in the hope that through my work I can help others as I have been helped myself.

I hope that you will feel the love that radiates from the intent and purpose of this book and that you will continue to do so.

Liz x

For more information please visit my website: <u>www. sacredspacepage.co.uk</u>

Lightning Source UK Ltd.
Milton Keynes UK
UKOW05f2058280813

216133UK00001B/11/A